THE
ESSENTIAL
ADDICTION
RECOVERY
COMPANION

A WORKBOOK FOR THE MIND, BODY AND SOUL

RICHARD A. SINGER, JR.

Foreword by Jon Harcharek

Loving Healing Press

Ann Arbor, MI

The Essential Addiction Recovery Companion: A Guidebook for the Mind, Body, and Soul
Copyright © 2018 by Richard A. Singer, Jr. All Rights Reserved
For more information, please visit www.RickSingerBooks.com

ISBN 978-1-61599-402-1 paperback
ISBN 978-1-61599-403-8 eBook

Library of Congress Cataloging-in-Publication Data

Names: Singer, Richard A., author.
Title: The essential addiction recovery companion : a guidebook for the mind,
   body, and soul / by Richard A. Singer, Jr., MA ; foreword by Jon Harcharek.
Description: Ann Arbor, MI : Loving Healing Press, [2018].
Identifiers: LCCN 2018034344 (print) | LCCN 2018036014 (ebook) | ISBN
   9781615994038 (Kindle, ePub, pdf) | ISBN 9781615994021 (pbk. : alk. paper)
Subjects: LCSH: Addicts--Rehabilitation. | Substance abuse--Treatment.
Classification: LCC HV4998 (ebook) | LCC HV4998 .S5626 2018 (print) | DDC
   613.8--dc23
LC record available at https://lccn.loc.gov/2018034344

Published by
Loving Healing Press
5145 Pontiac Trail
Ann Arbor, MI 48105

www.LHPress.com
info@LHPress.com

Tollfree 888-761-6268 (USA/CAN)
Fax 734-663-6861

Distributed by Ingram Book Group (USA/CAN/AU), Bertram's Books (UK/EU)

Dedication

This book is dedicated to all human beings suffering in life.

May you find peace and joy one day at a time.

Author's Note

This guidebook is not a substitute for the treatment of addiction by a medical professional. Prior to beginning a program of recovery from addiction, it is often necessary to be treated medically for detoxification and initial stabilization, especially in the case of chemical substances and alcohol. Withdrawal from substances can be life threatening. If you have been drinking alcohol heavily or using drugs such as benzodiazepines, opiates, or stimulants, it is vital to consult with a medical professional before discontinuing the use of substances. Recovery is much more likely if you are medically detoxed and attend a rehabilitation program with the level of care necessary for your unique circumstances.

If you are currently experiencing a crisis, call 911.

Here are other specific numbers you can contact for help:

Treatment Hotline: 1-800-662-4357

Suicide Hotline: 1-800-273-8255

Contents

Foreword – A True story

I check myself into rehab, ready to tackle this thing once and for all. I'm studying the *AA Big Book*, memorizing all 12 Steps. I'm impatiently cramming for some "recovery exam," eager to prove I've been cured. And then I found a copy of *Eastern Wisdom, Western Soul.*

Was that the missing piece? Meditation? Being right here, right now? I ask my newly assigned therapist if it could be part of my treatment. Noticing my dog-eared paperback, he asks if I'd learned anything yet. "Yes," I answer breathlessly, "about taking things slowly."

"We'll work on slowing down together," he smiled. "I'm fairly familiar with that book anyway. I wrote it."

And that's Richard Singer for you. Wise. Helpful. Humble. With a special talent for simplifying life's challenges into positive lessons. His newest book—*The Essential Addiction Recovery Companion*—does exactly that, breaking down time-tested principles into achievable tips. You'll find something helpful on every page. With guidebook questions that hardly feel like work, they're more like discussions you should be having with yourself. There are inspiring quotes. Thoughts for the day. All in an easygoing voice reassuring you it's "ok."

So, congratulations. If you've read this far, you're clearly motivated to move forward. Take your time to learn from this book and this wise man. Even I did!

Jon Harcharek
Award-winning author & artist
Still working at being in the moment

Acknowledgements

It is difficult to acknowledge everyone that made this project possible because every human being I encountered helped me in some way. There's always those specific people who help directly in a positive way and those even more importantly who help you realize the person you DO NOT desire to be. I am a strong believer in the fact that our enemies are our greatest spiritual teachers thus, I must thank all those people in my life that show me the wrong way to live and truly motivate me to live in a genuine and humble manner. Thank you!

Specifically, I must thank my mother, father, sister, brother, Aunt Sandy, Uncle Wayne and my twin boys because if it wasn't for their presence and love I would have never made it out of my last relapse alive. They gave me a reason to fight and never give up while I was battling in the trenches of active addiction.

In addition, each and every one of the clients I worked with in the addiction field have inspired the completion of this guidebook and keep me going in the often very challenging field of addiction treatment. They may not realize it but each one of them teach me and help me much more than I could ever begin to help them.

Finally, there are two specific individuals that helped directly with this guidebook. I cannot thank them enough. Jon Harcharek was so kind to do a thorough edit and write the foreword. Victor Volkman continues to have faith in my work and does an amazing job as a publisher. Thank you from the bottom of my heart.

I must not forget to thank my loving and all powerful higher power, whatever and wherever you are. I am humbled, amazed and often confused by this mysterious power that I give all credit to because for some reason the words in this book bombarded my consciousness and continued to bombard my being until they were written. All my books were created in this way so I don't take much credit for anything I write. Thank you and I hope to continue and strengthen my relationship with YOU.

Rick Singer
Plains, Pennsylvania

Introduction

This guidebook is based on a previous book that I wrote titled, *101 Tips for Recovering from Addictions*. I wrote that book shortly after surviving a torturous 3-year relapse following 15 years of continuous recovery. It contains a detailed account of my personal story and the 101 strategies contained in this more in-depth guidebook.

When I survived that almost fatal experience I genuinely felt that I had to do something to help the human beings that continue to struggle with addiction out there on the battlefield. If you are an addict you know that it truly is a battlefield!

I've struggled with addiction in many forms since I was probably around 12 years old. Addiction has destroyed my entire life several times and has also given me a better life than I could imagine. I know this illness intimately and have extensive knowledge of the addictive mind and body. I've been in the trenches directly as an addict and as a treatment professional. My experience demonstrates that addiction will take you to the gates of insanity and death but more importantly that recovery is possible. I am a simple human being that has been devastated by addiction and given two distinct chances at life after being forced to my knees by this powerful illness.

This guidebook is a compilation of the most effective strategies I have used personally and professionally to transcend addiction. There are millions of human beings just like you and I that also use a combination of these strategies to live a better life free of the insanity of addiction. Please move forward and give yourself a break. As you probably know by now, addiction is a losing battle. I beg you to begin right this moment to make a decision and take action in order to experience the life that you and your loved ones deserve. May you transcend addiction and live a peaceful and joyous life one moment at a time.

How to Use This Guidebook

All the strategies and related questions compiled in this guidebook for recovery have been used and tested throughout years of successful recovery, relapse, and getting back into recovery again after three torturous years of addictive hell. Many of them have scientific evidence supporting them and have also been used by many of my patients in therapy over a twenty-year period. They are effective and I am positive that they will help you to create a new life, continue your recovery or help another human being transform their life. They simply just need to be applied with sincerity, persistence, willingness and an open mind.

How you use this book and the information within it is your choice. Perhaps perusing through it to read all the pages would be useful in the beginning and then maybe you can work on a page a day to work on growth in recovery. Or you may pick your favorites and start completing them immediately. Another way is to leave it up to chance, flip through the book and randomly stop when you feel it's right. If you are helping others, you may find it useful to assign a specific page you believe would help the most. Again, it is all your personal choice. I just hope that you will find this book helpful in some way. If it helps one human being suffering from addiction, then I've done my job.

Finally, no matter how you choose to use the book, please enjoy it and remain hopeful that there is a new life out there to be lived by you. One day at a time you will continue to grow and eventually pass it on to other human beings suffering the torment of their addictive illness.

I would love to talk to you about any comments, suggestions, or simply to have a conversation about life. I am always here so please reach out to me via my personal email - RSinger9999@gmail.com. Please visit www.RickSinger.org for up to date information.

Never, Never, Never give up on recovery!

Tip #1: Have Hope No Matter What!

"Only in the darkness can you see the stars."

Martin Luther King, Jr.

First and foremost, you must realize that there is hope for your recovery and a completely new life beyond your imagination. Millions of suffering addicts who were once considered hopeless and awaiting death enjoy a new life free from the agony and anguish of addiction. You are no different from these transformed individuals. If you have breath in your body you possess hope. Now is the time to fight for what you deeply desire. There can be no waiting. For many of us, there will be no tomorrow if we don't enter recovery today. Recovery and your new life want you exactly the way you are. So, let's get started on creating this miraculous new life.

Questions for Further Growth

Do you truly have hope inside you that you can change your life? Explain.

_____

_____

_____

_____

Do you believe that you deserve a better life and are worth it? Elaborate.

_____

_____

_____

_____

What makes you different from the millions of human beings that have gone from hopeless to living incredible lives?

_____

_____

_____

_____

Today is the day that you transform hope into action and begin transforming your life 24-hours at a time.

Tip #2: Find a Support Group Specifically for You

"Don't be shy about asking for help.
It doesn't mean you're weak, it only means you're wise."

Anonymous

Consider joining a program aimed at daily recovery or a support group focused on recovering from the type of addiction in your life. Be open minded and willing in this process. Recovery from addiction requires daily work which you will come to love and look forward to. There is no cure, however addiction can be eliminated from your life daily. There are tons of support groups, twelve-step groups and other programs that will fit your needs. Try one or try them all. You are bound to discover one that fits your unique needs. Do some research and give these groups a shot; you have nothing to lose and a new life to gain.

Questions for Further Growth

What do you have to lose when it comes to attending support group meetings? Can you make a commitment to give it a try?

_____

_____

_____

_____

What type of meetings or group do you think would fit your current situation?

_____

_____

_____

_____

Now take some action and do some research about support group meetings and write one or two down that you will attend immediately.

_____

_____

_____

_____

Today I will be open-minded and give myself a break. I will make a commitment to attend a meeting of my choice.

Tip #3: Begin to Trust

"The best way to find out if you can trust somebody is to trust them."
Ernest Hemingway

Trust plays a major part in many aspects of recovery; thus, it is vital that we develop trust in others to accept help and develop intimate relationships. It's amazing how many of us blindly trusted drug dealers and other addicted "friends" then when we enter recovery, we don't want to trust anyone. Take a risk and trust people who want to help you until they give you a reason not to. Believe it or not, there are many genuine people out there who want to help us. Finally, try to go a step further and trust a power greater than yourself. This can be nature, your higher self, the universe, or perhaps a creator, if you believe in one. You will be amazed how influential trust can be in your recovery.

Questions for Further Growth

Do you have people in your life that you trust?

_____

_____

_____

_____

Are there any major events in your life that may have affected your trust for people or life in general?

_____

_____

_____

_____

Do you trust yourself?

_____

_____

_____

_____

Today, I will take a risk and begin trusting someone or something.

Tip #4: Take It Easy

"Adopt the pace of nature: her secret is patience."

Ralph Waldo Emerson

Take things slow. You are in this for the long haul. Long-term recovery depends on taking one day and one step at a time. You have plenty of time to achieve all your goals and create the life you desire. Don't stress yourself out and rush the process. You are exactly where you need to be at the current time. All great accomplishments are completed with one small achievable goal at a time and your #1 priority is to remain in recovery. The rest will fall into place, I promise. Relax and know that everything is going to be okay.

Questions for Further Growth

What would make your life perfect right this moment? (Visualize your ideal life.)

_____

_____

_____

_____

It is very normal to want everything in life to come all at once. However, reality tells us we must wait and be patient. How does that feel to you?

_____

_____

_____

_____

What are some things you are having a hard time practicing patience about in recovery?

_____

_____

_____

_____

_____

_____

Today I will build the foundation for my success one step at a time.

Tip #5: No Cravings?

"Addiction can deceive you in many ways:
one blatant and fatal lie is that you have been spontaneously cured."

Richard A. Singer Jr.

Many people right out of treatment or early in recovery are amazed that they have no desire to get high, drunk, or engage in whatever addiction they have. This is a wonderful thing; be grateful for it and enjoy it, but don't let it fool you. You will get the obsession again or at least a craving and you must be prepared for this reality. Right now, it may be the furthest thing from your mind, but in a split second the obsession can bombard you and take over your entire being. Develop a plan to deal with cravings when they surprise you!

Questions for Further Growth

Who are some people you can call if you do get the sudden desire to engage in addictive behavior?

_____

_____

_____

_____

Are there places or people you can avoid that may trigger an unnecessary craving?

_____

_____

_____

_____

What are some thoughts you can use to challenge addictive thoughts?

_____

_____

_____

_____

_____

*Today, I will realize that if a craving does come
I do not have to fall prey to it.*

Tip #6: Cravings Come and Go

"I am one drug away from never being clean again for the rest of my life."

Unknown

There are many strategies for overcoming cravings. First, know that the craving will end whether you give in to it or not. You will not die from a craving nor do you have to engage in the addictive behavior. Here are several strategies for emergency situations: *1. Offer help to someone in need. 2. Distract yourself with an enjoyable activity. 3. Take a hot or cold shower. 4. Eat something sweet 5. Don't fight or resist it. 6. Allow it to flow through you. 7. Exercise intensely 8. Call someone and talk it through.* Cravings do not last very long if we do not feed them. The more we focus on the craving, the stronger it gets. Allow the craving to come and go and you will realize how much stronger you become when you are on the other side. These strategies do work if you are persistent and dedicated. Remember the life you desire; addiction has no place in it.

Questions for Further Growth

What are some things that may trigger a craving to occur for you personally?

_____

_____

_____

_____

What are the most effective strategies you have used against cravings?

_____

_____

_____

_____

What are some thoughts you can use to challenge your cravings?

_____

_____

_____

_____

*Today I will be confident and know that if a craving comes
I will get through it no matter what.*

Tip #7: Is It Worth It?

"My worst day sober is better than my best day in addiction."

Unknown

A strategy that works very well for me when I am in a funk or just want to escape is asking myself if that short moment of euphoria is worth the long-term consequences and pain. Getting high for me lasts a very short while and then I find myself in a mental hospital, police station, or homeless and penniless. The little high I get from drinking, gambling, smoking crack or shooting dope is not worth giving up the unbelievable life I have. Death is the inevitable and final consequence but the deep pain of existence that results from addiction is what sucks.

Questions for Further Growth

Is the momentary high worth your family, friends and all you truly care about in life?

_____

_____

_____

_____

What are some of your thoughts about the battle you have been engaged in with your addiction?

_____

_____

_____

_____

_____

What are some of the feelings that addiction covers up for you?

_____

_____

_____

_____

_____

Today I will choose life over the destruction that my addiction causes.

Tip #8: Ask for Help!

"The only mistake you can make is not asking for help."

Sandeep Jauhar

Whatever you do in your recovery I beg you to not do it alone. I've walked that prideful and lonely road before. Get rid of the faulty belief that asking for help is weak; reaching out for help is one of the wisest and most courageous things we can do. Nothing worthwhile in life can be done alone. All great achievements were the product of a team of individuals supporting each other and recovery is no different. Just imagine the infinite possibilities and the countless number of people you will help. Not to mention what your family and friends will feel. Please ask for help! People want to support and help you recover from this sinister illness. Our connection to others and the world around us is one of the most vital steps we must take if we are to free ourselves from addiction. Addiction feeds on loneliness and despair so we must starve it by staying connected.

Questions for Further Growth

What holds you back from reaching out for help? (i.e. feelings, thoughts, beliefs?)

_____

_____

_____

_____

Do you have people in your life that you can ask for help?

_____

_____

_____

_____

What are some things you currently need help with?

_____

_____

_____

_____

Today I will allow myself to be vulnerable and ask for help.

Tip #9: Do Some Research

"Gain knowledge. It's valuable."

Daniel Norris

Do some research on addiction. Gaining knowledge and insight about the nature of addiction can help you accept and understand yourself a little better. Just choose the information you research wisely. There are many things online that are not very accurate and can be misleading. The more you understand the better you will feel about your recovery. Don't we always try to become educated about things we are passionate about and want to thrive in? Why not become knowledgeable about your life or death condition?

Questions for Further Growth

What is the formal definition of addiction per the American Society of Addiction Medicine? (www.ASAM.org)

_____

_____

_____

_____

What are some important things that you would like to know about addiction and how it affects you?

_____

_____

_____

_____

Research some books about addiction that you can commit to read as part of your recovery. List them below

_____

_____

_____

_____

Today I will take responsibility to learn about the illness that threatens my life.

Tip #10: Goodbye Letter

"If you are brave enough to say goodbye, life will reward you with a new hello."

Paulo Coelho

Personally, I required closure at the end of my addiction and the beginning of my new life. Addiction was a huge part of my life and I needed to say farewell, much like losing a horrible girlfriend who offered great sex occasionally. I also used this with many patients I treated in the past in both inpatient and outpatient settings. The letter has helped many people come to terms with the loss. Start out by writing, *Dear Addiction*, or whatever you wish to call it, then write anything and everything you think, believe, and feel about leaving your addiction behind. You may have mixed feelings and that is certainly normal. Do not worry about grammar and do not censor your writing. Let it flow from your heart and soul.

Questions for Further Growth

What feelings surface when you think about leaving the relationship with your addiction?

_____

_____

_____

_____

Are you willing to say goodbye? *Be honest! It's okay if you do not feel ready. Write this in your letter.*

_____

_____

_____

_____

Who are you going to process and share this letter with?

_____

_____

_____

_____

Today, I will say Good Bye to the deadly beast
that took everything from me.

Tip #11: Welcome Letter

"Imagine your ideal future. Visualize yourself as if your life were perfect in every respect."
Brian Tracy

Let's build on the previous tip and write a letter saying hello to your newfound recovery. Again, simply express what is in your heart. You can express your thoughts about recovery, your fears, your dreams, and your aspirations. Most importantly, be honest and sincere. I find it helpful to share these letters with family, friends, therapists, and anyone involved in your new life. Perhaps you want to share it online or in a support group. It's all up to you but make sure you write it. Use the questions below to get ideas for your letter.

Questions for Further Growth

What are your initial feelings when you think about your new life in recovery?

_____

_____

_____

_____

_____

Do you have dreams or goals you want to accomplish that you once thought of as a child?

_____

_____

_____

_____

_____

What type of person do you want to become?

_____

_____

_____

_____

_____

Today I will embrace my new life and visualize accomplishing all my dreams and aspirations.

Tip #12: Relapse is not a Requirement

"Sometimes relapse doesn't seem like that much of a threat.
But nobody is guaranteed to live through their next one."

Josie Tuttle

Relapse occurs in the recovery process; however, it is certainly not a necessity. The dangerous part of relapse is that there is no guarantee that we will make it back alive. If you do relapse and make it back, like myself, make sure you learn from it and appreciate another shot at recovery. It is almost like a rebirth because it is so easy to die when we unleash the monster of addiction again. Realistically, millions of individuals never even get one chance at treatment or recovery and there are the unfortunate ones who do not get another chance after a relapse. As we know, addiction either kills us or we end up in prison. There truly are no other options.

Questions for Further Growth

What are your sincere thoughts about relapse?

_____

_____

_____

_____

What would you gain from relapsing that you don't currently have now?

_____

_____

_____

_____

Visualize briefly what a relapse would look like and write it down?

_____

_____

_____

_____

Today I will be grateful for the 24 hours I have and realize that some people never get the opportunity that I have right in front of me.

Tip #13: Unbreakable

"You will not be the same after the storms of life:
you will be stronger, wiser and more alive than ever before."

Bryant McGill

We are much like trees weathering a storm. Our branches and leaves may shake and be wrathfully blown around, but we have a calm, still, and steady place within us that allows us to stay strong and survive. Discover this place of stillness and allow it to keep you sturdy and stable during the storms of life. We all possess this calm center within; it just takes some searching to discover it. Once revealed, it is always there for you to deal with the turbulence of life.

Questions for Further Growth

What storms have you survived in the past and how did it feel coming out on the other side?

_____

_____

_____

_____

_____

What would happen if you simply observed the storms going on around you and didn't act?

_____

_____

_____

_____

_____

Are there people around you that have gone through similar situations that you can reach out to?

_____

_____

_____

_____

_____

Today I will stand tall with my head up and know that I can get through anything that comes my way.

Tip #14: D-E-N-I-A-L

"We refuse to see how bad something is until it completely destroys us."

Unknown

Don't Even kNow I Am Lying is what this word stands for and clearly explains what the word represents. Denial is the most powerful and devious aspect of addiction. We clearly create lies and manipulate ourselves and don't even consciously realize we are doing it. This is the epitome of deceit. If we fail to gain awareness of these lies we will remain sick at the core of our being and ultimately end up deep within active addiction without even realizing how we got there. We must stop believing the lies and falling prey to the manipulation of addiction. Recovery is about aligning with the truth and living it daily.

Questions for Further Growth

What are some of the lies that you consistently tell yourself?

_____

_____

_____

_____

Are you ready to be completely honest with yourself and face reality 100%?

_____

_____

_____

_____

Who are some supportive people in your life that you can ask to confront you on your lies when they see you feeding the monster of DENIAL in your head?

_____

_____

_____

_____

Today I will connect with people who can call me on my bullshit otherwise known as DENIAL.

Tip #15: Surrender to Win

"The moment of surrender is not when life is over. It's when it begins."
Marianne Williamson

You will receive endless advice when it comes to recovery. People like to just spout things out like it is a simple process. One of these suggestions will likely be, "Just Surrender." Well that sounds wonderful but it's certainly not as easy as "Just Surrendering." Surrender for me means to completely let go of control and trust that everything is going to work out. Once I do this, I can resign as the CEO of the universe and get out of my own way. When I surrender, I picture myself throwing up my hands and stating, "I give up! Please guide me on my journey." Try it!

Questions for Further Growth

What do you believe you have control of in your life?

_____

_____

_____

_____

Think back a little on most of your plans. Did they really work out exactly the way you wanted them to?

_____

_____

_____

_____

Have you ever tried to simply let go and live life a different way? What do you really have to lose at the moment? Give it a try!

_____

_____

_____

_____

Today I will throw my hands up and let go of control completely.

Tip #16: Daily Plan

"Your future depends of the choices you make today.
The future for this reason can be predicted by your day-to-day living."

Israelmore Ayivor

I like to have a plan for the day. I usually do this the night before. It helps provide structure to my day so I don't get caught up and lost in the chaos of the world. Of course, I realize that plans don't usually go "as planned," so I am very mindful of being flexible and taking the day as it presents itself to me. There's a saying I like to remember, "If you want to make the universe laugh at you, make plans." That's very relevant in my life, but having a rough draft for the day to come does help me.

Questions for Further Growth

What aspects of your day do you believe you should plan? (i.e. meetings, appointments, etc.)

_____

_____

_____

_____

_____

What feelings do you have about having a blueprint for your day to come? Any feelings holding you back from taking this important step?

_____

_____

_____

_____

Start now! Write a plan for today and make sure you get a small journal and anything else you may need to make this a small effective habit in your daily journey.

_____

_____

_____

_____

_____

Today I will begin creating a daily plan for my new life.

Tip #17: Daily Inventory

"Practice the philosophy of continuous improvement. Get a little better every single day."
Unknown

I've developed the habit of reviewing how my day went in the evening when I'm ready to go to bed. I simply review my day and assess what I did well, if I hurt anyone throughout the day, and what I could possibly do better in the future. I keep it very simple and use this strategy to remain conscious of my actions and not live on auto pilot like I did in my addiction. Let's try it NOW and in the future, you can use the questions below as a guide to take an inventory of your day.

Questions for Further Growth

Did I do my best today in all situations? If not where can I make improvements?

_____

_____

_____

_____

_____

Did I hurt anyone intentionally or without realizing it? If so how can I make amends immediately?

_____

_____

_____

_____

Did I reach out to help at least one person? Who and how will I help another human being at the next opportunity?

_____

_____

_____

_____

Today I will remember that I do not have to be perfect
I just have to make progress.

Tip #18: You are NOT Your Mind

"The hardest prison to escape is in your mind."

Unknown

Addiction lives and thrives within our minds. We are not our mind so we must choose to get the hell out of there. Many people live their lives believing they are their mind and completely identify themselves with this devious creature. If we are going to create a new life, we must begin to identify with and live according to our heart. Your heart is where your genuine self resides. Our addiction cannot survive if we choose to live our lives with the guidance of our heart. Always remember that addiction is in the mind and recovery is in the heart.

Questions for Further Growth

Have you searched your heart for the truth about your addiction? What does it tell you?

_____

_____

_____

_____

How has your mind taken you down the wrong path in the past? Give specific examples.

_____

_____

_____

_____

_____

Ask your heart these vital questions and listen closely: Am I an addict?; Where do I truly want to be in my life?; What do I need to do to live fully and at peace?

_____

_____

_____

_____

_____

*Today I will begin to travel the road from my mind
to my heart and trust my heart just a little more.*

Tip #19: Our Wonderful Forgetter

"You can't make the same mistake twice. The second time you make
the mistake, it's no longer a mistake it becomes a choice."

Unknown

Our "Addicted Brain" has the incredible ability to forget all the destructive and horrid consequences we have experienced in our active addiction. If we allow ourselves to forget the consequences of addiction, we are bound to end up back in that hell. Amazingly, your mind can even convince you that relapsing is a great idea. So, the more detailed and emotionally stimulating your list is, the better it is when your addiction decides to play these mind games again. After answering the questions below write a detailed description of the things you don't want to forget and look back at this so you NEVER have to experience these consequences or feel this way again.

Questions for Further Growth

What are some ways you have been a completely different person when under the spells of your addiction?

_____

_____

_____

_____

How have you hurt the people who truly love and care about you?

_____

_____

_____

_____

Visualize the worst feelings you have experienced in your addiction and describe those in detail.

_____

_____

_____

_____

*Today I will not live based on my past, but I will remember where I do not
want to ever go back to.*

Tip #20: You are Not a Victim!

"When you complain, you make yourself a victim.
Leave the situation, change the situation or accept it. All else is madness."

Eckhart Tolle

Personally, there was a period when I sincerely felt like the ultimate victim of my addiction. This completely sabotaged any possible chance of recovery. This frame of mind resulted in utter hopelessness and I had no capacity to reach out for help or help myself in any way. I became doomed to the destruction and ultimate death associated with my addiction. There is absolutely no possibility of creating a better life when we see ourselves as a victim. We have hope and a choice. There are millions who have transcended addiction and you are no different than any of those human beings. You must discard the victim mentality right now and take action. There is no time for delay.

Questions for Further Growth

Do you feel like a victim of your addiction? Explain and express this.

_____

_____

_____

_____

Do you have any feelings inside of you that can help you escape these feelings of hopelessness?

_____

_____

_____

_____

What and who gives you hope that you can recover?

_____

_____

_____

_____

Today I will transcend victimhood and internalize the fact that I have the power to treat my addiction daily.

Tip #21: Crossing the Line

"The idea that somehow, someday he will control and enjoy his drinking is the great obsession of every abnormal drinker. The persistence of this illusion is astonishing. Many pursue it into the gates of insanity or death."

Alcoholics Anonymous Big Book

Somewhere in your life you crossed the line of "normal" use or behavior into the bottomless pit of addiction. Make no mistake, once this line is crossed there is no going back. It's often said, "Once you become a pickle you will never go back to being a cucumber." Many addicts, including myself, hold onto the great delusion that we will somehow, someday go back to "social" use. If you continue to allow this belief in your life it will destroy you. This thought and belief must be smashed and thrown away right now.

Questions for Further Growth

Write down some specific delusional thoughts that your mind incessantly holds onto?

_____

_____

_____

_____

Challenge these thoughts with facts from your experience?

_____

_____

_____

_____

What feelings continue to act as obstacles to accepting the obvious fact that you cannot control your addiction?

_____

_____

_____

_____

Today I will not feed the delusions of addiction;
I will focus on reality and what I can do to recover.

Tip #22: The Placebo Effect

"In any project the important factor is your belief.
Without belief, there can be no successful outcome."

William James

The Placebo Effect demonstrates the power of belief. It refers to something being effective because we believe it is going to be effective. The Placebo Effect can be utilized in so many ways. A whole book can easily be written about it and probably has, though for our use right now, we can focus on tapping into its power concerning the recovery process. Begin to truly believe in your new life free from all addictions. Stop saying and believing you are hopeless. There are tons of great resources out there that you need to begin tapping into. BELIEVE and all things are possible

Questions for Further Growth

What are some faulty beliefs that may hold you back in recovery?

_____

_____

_____

_____

How have positive and negative beliefs affected your life in the past? Have your beliefs come true in certain areas of your life whether positive or negative?

_____

_____

_____

_____

What are some core beliefs that can help you transform your life and act as motivators to make this transformation a reality?

_____

_____

_____

_____

_____

Today I will truly believe in the incredible life I can build in recovery.

Tip #23: Allow People to Help You

"Give, but give until it hurts."

Mother Teresa

I came to realize this incredibly helpful concept when watching the movie *90 Minutes in Heaven*. The main character was fatally depressed and gave up all hope in his life. He wouldn't let his family or friends help him until he suddenly realized that letting others help him helped them even more. We need to allow others the gift of helping us.

Questions for Further Growth

What is holding you back from allowing other human beings to help you? Is it pride, selfishness, etc.?

_____

_____

_____

_____

_____

What do you really have to lose when it comes to reaching out for help or allowing yourself to be vulnerable enough to accept help?

_____

_____

_____

_____

_____

What feelings do you get when you help others? Do you really want to deprive others the positive feelings associated with being helpful to another human being?

_____

_____

_____

_____

_____

Today I will realize that allowing others to help me often helps them more than I can ever know.

Tip #24: Express Yourself

"Unexpressed emotions will never die.
They are buried alive and will come forth later in uglier ways."

Sigmund Freud

Addiction wants you to keep everything hidden within your murky mind. Doing this will ultimately lead to an implosion and, eventually, an explosion. It's also extremely self-abusive. We must get this stuff out of the crazy carnival we have going on in our heads. We can share our thoughts and emotions with others, write them down, talk with the universe or our higher power, or use any strategy we are comfortable with. Whatever you choose to do, make sure everything gets out of your head. It's a dangerous place! We must release our thoughts and emotions into the light and discover the truth and solutions necessary to deal with life.

Questions for Further Growth

What are some thoughts and feelings that overwhelm you?

_____

_____

_____

_____

What prevents you from letting these thoughts and feelings out into the light?

_____

_____

_____

_____

What are some ways you feel comfortable expressing your inner most thoughts and feelings? Start slow and you will begin to feel the freedom that comes from expression.

_____

_____

_____

_____

Today I will release my thoughts and feelings into the light so I can experience peace and joy in my heart.

Tip #25: Recovery is for People Who Want It Bad

"There is implanted in every man, naturally, a strong desire for progress."

Swami Vivekananda

My recovery from addiction is the greatest gift I was ever given and it was free. However, it was not given to me when I needed it, which would have been long before I created my new life. It was given to me when I genuinely desired it with all my heart and soul. I had to be willing to do anything and everything to get it and keep it daily. It's not much different than addiction when I was willing to go to any lengths to get what I needed to function. You will see that the frame of mind of recovery and addiction are not much different at all; they are just simply transferred from negative and self-destructive to positive and constructive. We have everything we need to create a new life just like we had all the skills necessary to survive in addiction. We are some of the most intelligent, creative and unbelievably strong people.

Questions for Further Growth

Are you sincerely ready to go to any lengths for freedom?

_____

_____

_____

_____

Is there something holding you back from an all-out effort?

_____

_____

_____

_____

What are some skills you demonstrated in your addiction that can be positively utilized in recovery?

_____

_____

_____

_____

Today I will do everything in my power to move forward in my recovery and my personal growth.

Tip #26: Narcissism-Beware!

"Narcissistic people are always struggling with the
fact that the rest of the world doesn't revolve around them."

Unknown

Beware of personality characteristics related to narcissism. I know it's a strong word but if you're honest with yourself you will probably notice these characteristics in your life. I know I certainly did. These characteristics are things like thinking we are above others, rules don't apply to us, using people as objects, and other selfish behaviors that we demonstrated in our addictions. This is the frame of mind that the universe revolves around us and is very ego based and immature. This mind set is very hazardous to our recovery and our quality of life. Change in this area is imperative.

Questions for Further Growth

If you are brutally honest with yourself, what are some narcissistic thoughts and behaviors that manifest in your life?

_____

_____

_____

_____

Now look back and think about where these traits have gotten you. What were some specific consequences for these characteristics?

_____

_____

_____

_____

List one specific narcissistic trait you possess and how you will work on changing that today.

_____

_____

_____

_____

Today I will get out of the "Great I am" and become part of humanity.

Tip #27: Put Yourself Out There

"Reciprocity is a deep instinct; it is the basic currency of social life."

Jonathan Haidt

Your social life is not over when you enter recovery, in fact, it has just begun. If you were anything like me in your addiction, you were not a social genius, especially toward the end. Recovery allows us the benefit and gift of developing genuine relationships with mutual love and care. I've learned unconditional love and respect in my new relationships. Open up and become willing to make connections. You will discover a new desire for intimate connection and involvement in society. It will no longer be all about you and your needs. A whole new world will appear and you will be a unique and productive part of it.

Questions for Further Growth

What fears and obstacles face you when you think about connecting with people in recovery?

_____

_____

_____

_____

_____

What defines a healthy social relationship for you?

_____

_____

_____

_____

_____

What are some of the social skills you may feel that you struggle with?

_____

_____

_____

_____

Today I will give back to humanity and become
involved as a productive human being.

Tip #28: Diverse Brain Chemistry

"Drug addiction is not a choice of lifestyle,
it is a disorder of the brain and we need to recognize this."

Unknown

As human beings suffering from addiction, our brain chemistry is unlike other people. There are many recent scientific studies demonstrating many differences in the addicted brain. I suggest you do a little research to see what science is discovering for yourself. There are still a lot of unknowns in the field of addiction, nevertheless we are making great advances. The reality is that the neuro-chemical properties of our brain change through recovery. If we stick out the process, we make great strides in forming new neuronal connections and paths that override the old ones. This is referred to as plasticity and is absolutely amazing. Recovery helps to rewire your brain for success.

Questions for Further Growth

What would you like to research further about your brain chemistry?

_____

_____

_____

_____

What new behaviors are you experimenting with in recovery that will help you to rewire your brain?

_____

_____

_____

_____

When you realize that your brain chemistry is different from the non-addict what feelings or thoughts come up for you?

_____

_____

_____

_____

*Today I will recognize that I have an illness involving
the brain that needs daily treatment to remain in remission.*

Tip #29: PAWS – Post -Acute Withdrawal Syndrome

"You have to fight through some bad days to earn the best days of your life."

Unknown

Post-Acute Withdrawal Syndrome can last months to years after we stop using or engaging in addictive behavior. Feeling like you are going through withdrawal all over again during recovery is not abnormal and you can survive it. The more you do for your recovery the better your outcome will be. Some of the major symptoms include but are not limited to the following: mood swings, anxiety, irritability, tiredness, variable energy, low enthusiasm, variable concentration, and disturbed sleep. Develop a plan to manage these symptoms and you will transcend the prison of addiction.

Questions for Further Growth

Do you believe you are currently experiencing symptoms of PAWS? If so what symptoms?

_____

_____

_____

_____

_____

_____

_____

What is your individualized strategy to monitor and manage PAWS in your recovery?

_____

_____

_____

_____

_____

_____

_____

_____

*Today I will allow the feelings of recovery to flow through
me and know that they are all a normal part of growth.*

Tip #30: Impatience is Not a Virtue

"Don't go back to less just because you're too inpatient to wait for more."

Unknown

I don't know about you but impatience and a lack of tolerance are two of my major problems. I want everything right now and I want it my way. In addition, I want people to act the way I do and the way I want them to act. If these things don't happen I normally get very irritated. Unfortunately, this is certainly not how life works. We need to look at this area of our inner self and work on changing these attitudes a little at a time. Practicing patience with ourselves, other people, and situations is imperative in recovery. Once I made these changes and altered my perception, my life became much more pleasant.

Questions for Further Growth

What areas of your life are you most impatient and intolerant?

_____

_____

_____

_____

What are some thought patterns that need to change in regards to accepting people as people?

_____

_____

_____

_____

When you notice yourself being impatient with life what are some strategies that you can use right in the moment?

_____

_____

_____

_____

_____

Today I will practice patience and tolerance with myself and others.

Tip #31: Start Your Day Over at Any Time or Sit in Your Shit?

"The only real battle in life is between hanging on and letting go."

Shannon L. Alder

No matter what is going on in your day and how dreadful it becomes always keep in mind that you can start it over at any time. The first time I read this in a book I had a profound awakening. We possess this power and this choice in our lives. We can continue to wallow in the misery of the day or start over and make it calm and joyous. It's completely up to you. Maybe you like to stay in the misery and drama, but I certainly do not anymore. Especially drama, I stay as detached from this as I possibly can. No more being drawn into people's nightmares for me. It is simply amazing how much freedom and power we receive when we surrender from addiction and choose a life of recovery. Just try it out for a while and you will be hooked.

Questions for Further Growth

Does it help you to focus on the negative throughout your day?

_____

_____

_____

_____

What are some ways you can initiate a "do-over" when you're having a bad day?

_____

_____

_____

_____

Do you feel more comfortable in drama and chaos then in peace? Why?

_____

_____

_____

_____

_____

Today I will utilize the strategy of starting over rather than staying stuck.

Tip #32: Embrace the Mystery

"The most beautiful thing we can experience is the mysterious.
It is the source of all true art and science."

Albert Einstein

My life was always filled with analyzing, obsessing, and trying to figure everything out. I needed to know everything and challenge whatever people told me. Thinking critically and gaining knowledge is certainly not a bad thing, but there are things in this universe that we will never figure out. In fact, no matter how much we know and learn, we will always only know a speck of the available information. At some point, we must recognize this fact and begin to embrace the mystery of our existence and all its miracles.

Questions for Further Growth

What do you find to be miraculous and mysterious about this universe?

_____

_____

_____

_____

What fears do you have when it comes to simply embracing and enjoying life for what it is?

_____

_____

_____

_____

What are some things you can do to help with the need for control or having all the answers?

_____

_____

_____

_____

_____

Today I will embrace the beautiful mystery that life truly is.

Tip #33: Feel Your Feelings and Move Forward

"Feelings are just visitors. Let them come and go."

Mooji

We are human and that means we will experience a diverse spectrum of feelings. This can sometimes seem like an incredible gift and sometimes feel like an evil curse. We often try to go around or avoid the feelings we don't like. That's very normal. One fact about all human beings is that we attempt to maximize pleasure and minimize pain. However, the fact remains that we must go directly through our feelings to deal with them rather than let our feelings deal with us. An author friend of mine, Nancy Gilbertson, calls this, "Constructive Wallowing" in her new book. She states that, "We must allow our true feelings into awareness, name them, and give ourselves a hug." Basically, we need to make friends with our feelings; they are not going to kill us, but if we stuff them they may lead to dangerous behavior. Stop judging your feelings and simply allow yourself to feel them and move forward in your life.

Questions for Further Growth

What are some specific feelings that you struggle with daily?

_____

_____

_____

_____

Pick one of these feelings and describe it in detail?

_____

_____

_____

_____

Who can you begin to process these feelings with?

_____

_____

_____

_____

Today I will sit with my feelings and simply feel them without having to judge or take any action.

Tip #34: Do the Next Right Thing

"Do the right thing. It will gratify some people and astonish the rest."

Mark Twain

One of the most effective strategies in my own recovery is the simple and almost thoughtless act of doing the next right thing. Move forward each moment and do what you know in your heart to be correct. This works well when I'm overwhelmed and have no clue where to turn or what to do. Amazingly, life comes together by simply following this plan. It's quite transformative and much different than how we acted in our addicted life. For me, it kind of warms my heart and makes me feel respectable to do what is right and be a "normal" member of society. Believe me, I couldn't always say this.

Questions for Further Growth

How can you tell the difference between right behavior and risky behavior?

_____

_____

_____

_____

_____

_____

When you're doing the right things in your life what kind of feelings do you experience?

_____

_____

_____

_____

_____

_____

_____

_____

Today I will be guided by that little voice inside
that knows what is right and what is wrong.

Tip #35: Perception is Everything

"What is behind your eyes holds more power than what is in front of them."

Gary Zukav

Perception is the lens we see the totality of life through. It has a powerful impact on our thoughts, beliefs, and behavior. In recovery, our perception must change. We must begin transforming our view of our self and the world in a more realistic and effective manner. This will begin to happen as we change our thinking from self-centered to asking what we can add to the world around us. I know self-centered is a harsh word but if you look honestly at addiction in general, it changes our mind to focus on what we need to do for "me". So, I'm certainly not saying that the core of your being is selfish, but the addictive illness does make us that way. Change your perception and your whole outlook on life will change.

Questions for Further Growth

What overall perceptive pattern in your life needs to change? (For example, negativity, pessimism, victimhood, etc.)

_____

_____

_____

_____

_____

Write down one specific perception you have that doesn't serve you well.

_____

_____

_____

_____

How can this perception be challenged in a productive way?

_____

_____

_____

_____

Today I see life through the lens of the spirit.

Tip #36: Journaling from the Soul

"Whether you're keeping a journal or writing as a meditation, it's the same thing.
What's important is that your having a relationship with your mind."

Natalie Goldberg

Writing down our thoughts, feelings, and behaviors each day is a tremendous strategy to monitor our progress, search deep within ourselves, and stay out of our damn head. Journaling has been thoroughly researched and shown to be a very effective strategy for self-growth and transformation. Simply jotting down what's going on within you without judgment or worrying about making sense is enormously healing. I found it to be so effective in early recovery that I ended up writing a daily meditation book with journaling sections basically just to help myself, though writing a book was also a major goal of mine. Try it for a short period and you will realize how good it feels to get things out of your mind and down on paper. Also, check out my journaling book *Your Daily Walk with the Great Minds* if you get a chance. Had to plug it there; it was perfect timing. Lol. You can contact me and I'll send you a free review copy of the journal for your personal recovery use.

Questions for Further Growth

What holds you back from keeping a daily journal?

_____

_____

_____

_____

Experiment with journaling right now! What thoughts, feelings, and behaviors have you experienced today?

_____

_____

_____

_____

_____

_____

_____

Today I will begin a journaling adventure to
deeply connect with my deepest self.

Tip #37: Rationalizing is Our Game

"Rationalization may be defined as self-deception by reasoning."

Unknown

"To Thine Own Self Be True." This saying is a precise description of the new life we are creating. Self-honesty is the key. Rationalizing is the one thing that prevents us from this vital act. Deep down we know the truth, but justifying things conceals the truth from our being and eventually causes self-destruction. I can rationalize the hell out of anything. I can make myself believe anything in my own mind. I had to put an abrupt end to this in recovery. I had to face the harsh truth of reality and accept it for what is was. Rationalizing was my greatest defense mechanism for most of my life. However, I realized that it could easily sabotage my recovery. I was a master of fabricating and believing my own lies. This completely blocked me from living a genuine and authentic life so it had to be thrown out of my repertoire.

Questions for Further Growth

What are some specific rationalizations that you use regularly?

_____

_____

_____

_____

How has the use of rationalization affected you in the past?

_____

_____

_____

_____

What is one truth about your life that you need to accept completely to recover?

_____

_____

_____

_____

Today I will face reality head on without using
the defense mechanism of rationalization.

Tip #38: Always Help Others, No Matter What

"Only a life lived for others is a life worthwhile."

Albert Einstein

Recovery is about getting healthy, being a productive part of society, and helping others. Life makes much more sense and is much more joyous when we are giving of ourselves. We all have a unique purpose in this universe based on our passions and talents and this always aligns with helping others in some way. We are social animals and need each other to survive and prosper. Helping people adds meaning and purpose to our lives and strengthens our intimate connection to humanity. Get out there and see what you can do for others. It will keep you out of yourself and will give you infinite gifts. I guarantee that nobody ever felt dissatisfied or unhappy when they helped someone else. Simple things create great joy within me. Just today I was in a small corner store paying for coffee and I told the cashier to charge me for two and give the next person a coffee for free. This gave me intense pleasure and it was a very simple act.

Questions for Further Growth

Do you spend a great deal of time focusing on how bad you feel?

_____

_____

_____

_____

What are some ways you can benefit the people around you?

_____

_____

_____

_____

What will you do today to get out of your own way and help another human being without telling anyone?

_____

_____

_____

_____

Today I will step out of myself and help others in any way possible.

Tip #39: Sleep is Vital

"The best bridge between despair and hope is a good night's sleep."

E. Joseph Cossman

Getting adequate sleep is vital for our mind, body, and spirit. Lack of sleep causes so many issues with our thinking, emotions, and wears down our spirit. The rejuvenation of all our cells happens during sleep. Your body will alert you when you need rest. Don't overwhelm and exhaust yourself. Listen to your body's wisdom; it has evolved over thousands of years and knows what is best for you. Sleep will make all the difference in your day and overall outlook on life.

Questions for Further Growth

Are you getting at least 6-8 hours of sleep at night?

_____

_____

_____

_____

Are you having difficulties falling asleep, staying asleep, or waking up rested?

_____

_____

_____

_____

What changes can you make in your day to ensure you are getting adequate rest?

_____

_____

_____

_____

_____

_____

_____

Today I will be aware of my body and its needs.

Tip #40: Repair the Past

"There is a vast difference between apologizing and making amends."

Unknown

Repairing the past is a huge step in the recovery process. We must make amends for the harm we caused and do our best to make it up to the people we hurt. This aspect of recovery was an enlightening experience for me. I felt free when I put an effort into mending the hurt that I caused. Before making amends, I was filled with guilt and shame for what I had done and this process truly relieved all that negativity. The key is to become willing and to work on this as diligently as possible. You don't have to do this all at once, and make sure you don't try doing it alone. Seek help from a therapist or someone else you know in recovery. We've said the word "sorry" so many times that it just doesn't cut it anymore. There's nothing genuine left in the word "Sorry." Make sure you have a strong foundation and do some research about the process. You will see that the act of being in recovery may be enough for many people you hurt, but still ask them what you can do to make it up to them.

Questions for Further Growth

Who can you reach out to help you with this vital and sensitive process?

_____
_____
_____
_____
_____
_____

Make a list of the people and the harms that you caused. Be thorough!

_____
_____
_____
_____
_____
_____
_____

Today I will begin taking the action needed
to repair my past the best I possibly can.

Tip #41: Therapy is Terrific

"The purpose of psychotherapy is to set people free."

Rollo May

I wholeheartedly believe that every human being should have a therapist in order to vent and get an objective view of their lives. And it's not just because I'm a therapist. I've been involved in therapy for 21 years and will be for the rest of my life. Therapy is an amazing gift! Always remember that you as the client or patient are always the customer and the therapist needs to be a good fit with you. This may take going to a few different therapists but you will eventually find an awesome one and will be grateful you did. Therapy offers you a chance to become intimate with yourself and discover the unlimited potential that resides within you. Give therapy a chance. It can transform your life.

Questions for Further Growth

What holds you back from working with a therapist regularly?

_____

_____

_____

_____

What are some traits you would like your therapist to possess?

_____

_____

_____

_____

What are some struggles a therapist may be able to help you with?

_____

_____

_____

_____

Today I will begin looking for a good therapist
as an additional weapon in my recovery arsenal.

Tip #42: You Must Have Fun

"It's kind of fun to do the impossible."

Walt Disney

Having fun and enjoying life is an essential part of recovery. It helps to develop a healthy mind, body, and spirit. Experiment with many activities to discover what you truly enjoy. We polluted ourselves for so long that we often forget what we enjoy and what fun is. Socializing with other people in recovery or people whose lives don't revolve around addiction is a great way to get involved in the things they are doing and enjoying. There are often picnics in the community, outdoor recreational activities, free workshops, concerts, drum circles, sports, road trips, and so on. I often look for activities in local papers and activity guides to find new spontaneous things to get involved in. Everything can actually be fun in recovery; however, you need to be open minded and patient. I know one thing for sure: my addiction was no longer any fun at all, it was pure torture. You have the power to create whatever you can imagine in your life.

Questions for Further Growth

What are some things that you have dreamed of doing as a child?

_____

_____

_____

_____

What is stopping you from being creative and attempting to make some of these dreams come true?

_____

_____

_____

_____

Begin making a bucket list of things you want to do in recovery.

_____

_____

_____

_____

Today I will integrate fun into everything I do.

Tip #43: Everything Must Change a Little at a Time

"Growth means change and change involves risk, stepping from the known to the unknown."
Unknown

There's a popular saying in treatment and many recovery communities that states, "If nothing changes, nothing changes." It's kind of the same as the definition of insanity which is doing the same thing repeatedly and expecting different results. Basically, if we don't change we will continue to do what we always did and get what we always got. That's insane, right? If you truly have the desire to escape your addiction, the answer is quite simple; you must change. We must change a lot, but not all at once. Change happens a day at a time and one step at a time. If you're willing to change and you're ready to act, you are well on your way. Remember, the great pyramids and many other astonishing creations were created one brick or one board or one stone at a time. It's all about persistently taking simple steps on a consistent basis. You got this!

Questions for Further Growth

What are some major things that you need to change in your recovery?

_____

_____

_____

_____

_____

_____

_____

List one of these changes and write down an initial strategy to begin this change today.

_____

_____

_____

_____

_____

_____

_____

Today I will work at changing one simple thing about me.

Tip #44: Sex Can Be Dangerous

"A shot to kill the pain. A pill to drain the shame. A purge to end the gain. A cut to break the vein. A smoke to ease the crave. A drink to win the game. An addiction is an addiction because it all hurts the same."

Unknown

This is one addiction you need to be aware of creeping up on you in early recovery. Sex and relationships can become very unhealthy obsessions and compulsions when we stop our addictive behavior. If you think about it, this is quite natural because sex and relationships can create an extremely addictive euphoric state like drugs, alcohol, and other behaviors. Just be mindful and aware of this when beginning recovery. On the other hand, even normal sex with your partner can be weird when you are in recovery, so be patient with yourself and communicate your feelings. Be mindful and aware of the potential risks and difficulties related to sex in recovery.

Questions for Further Growth

Have you had healthy sexual relationships in your life?

_____

_____

_____

_____

What are some criteria of a healthy relationship?

_____

_____

_____

_____

Are there sexual issues you need to process and work on in your recovery?

_____

_____

_____

_____

Today I will sincerely assess my relationships
and be sure I am not crossing the line into unhealthy behavior.

Tip #45: Give Yourself a Break, Please!

"Friendship with oneself is all important, because without it one cannot be friends with anyone else in the world."

Eleanor Roosevelt

If your addiction has been anything like mine, you have been through hell and literally tortured yourself. Recovery is a time for us to finally give ourselves a break at last and stop beating the shit out of our body. Seriously, stop torturing yourself and be gentle. This is your opportunity to create a new life with less pain and more joy. You do deserve it. Relax, breathe, and be kind to yourself.

Questions for Further Growth

Do you care about yourself enough to stop killing yourself with addiction?

_____

_____

_____

_____

Do you believe you are worth having a productive life?

_____

_____

_____

_____

_____

How will you be kind to yourself today?

_____

_____

_____

_____

_____

Today I will practice kindness toward myself.

Tip #46: Meditation is Helpful

"To understand the immeasurable, the mind must be extraordinarily quiet, still."
Jiddu Krishnamurti

Meditation is an incredibly powerful and effective tool in recovery. It is a universal calming method used to simply listen to the universe around you. It is not as complex as it's made out to be. Just sit and allow yourself to be still while letting your thoughts come and go quietly without judging or feeding into any of them. Just observe what is going on around you and within you. It is normal to try to meditate and find that your mind is a huge pain in the ass. That's just the nature of meditation. It will get easier and your mind will become calmer and quieter as you continue to practice. I suggest that you read a beginner's article or book and begin practicing it in your life for at least a few minutes each day. It's simply listening and witnessing rather than thinking and doing.

Questions for Further Growth

Have you ever tried meditation? If so what was your experience?

_____

_____

_____

_____

_____

_____

Try practicing stillness and silence for a few minutes. What was your experience?

_____

_____

_____

_____

_____

_____

Today I will commit to adding meditation to my daily recovery.

Tip #47: Prayer or Communication with the Universe

"The Simple Path. Silence is Prayer. Prayer is Faith.
Faith is Love. Love is Service. The Fruit of Service is Peace."

Mother Teresa

While meditation is listening, prayer is communication with whatever is out there. Whether you believe in a greater power beyond you or not, I would suggest talking to nature or just talking to your higher self. I talk to the universe many times a day. I truly have no idea what exists out there, but I do know that I am not the Ultimate. That would be a scary thing if I was. I thank the universe for allowing me to be alive and free from addiction. I ask for daily guidance and protection for my family and that's about it. I'm not into reciting special prayers because it's meaningless to me. I make my own special prayers which are always spontaneous, genuine, and sincere. If you don't believe or don't want to believe, simply talk to your higher self. The self that has infinite potential and always your best interest in mind. I truly believe there must be something that created everything within this perfect universe, but that's just me.

Questions for Further Growth

Do you believe that there is something more powerful than you?

_____

_____

_____

_____

_____

Write down some simple prayers that you can use daily to communicate with whatever you believe or understand?

_____

_____

_____

_____

_____

Today I will simply talk to something higher than myself.

Tip #48: Do the Opposite

"Many times in recovery it is very helpful to make yourself do what you really don't want to do."

Unknown

I overheard someone say years ago, that as addicts, our first thought is often wrong. This made complete sense to me. We know our first judgment or thought is often faulty but we play with these thoughts and eventually they begin to take us over resulting in rationalization. A good strategy to keep in mind when confronted with this way of thinking is to do the exact opposite of what your first though is. For example, if an old friend from my addiction texts me and says, "Why don't you just come and hang out with us? We haven't seen you in a while. You don't have to use anything we just want to see you." My first thought may be, "Yeah, you know what? They are right. I'll just hang out." Instead, I choose to act oppositely and call a friend who isn't actively addicted and go do something exciting. This works in many situations.

Questions for Further Growth

What are some negative and destructive thoughts that may pop in your head?

_____

_____

_____

_____

_____

_____

What are some opposing things you can think or do when this happens?

_____

_____

_____

_____

_____

_____

Today I will do something good for me that I really don't want to do.

Tip #49: Just 24 Hours

"Live one day at a time. Keep your attention in present time. Have no expectations. Make no judgements. And give up the need to know why things happen as they do. Give it up!"

Caroline Myss

Do not fall into the deceptive mind trap of constantly thinking, "I have to stay clean or in recovery forever." In early recovery, this mindset caused me panic attacks and led to many relapses. You simply need to stay away from your addiction for 24 hours. In all actuality, just for the moment. Take very small steps and they add up to big accomplishments. Focus on getting through the day and doing the next right thing. No addict stays sober or clean forever; they simply recover one day at a time. This reality makes life much more manageable and pleasurable, after all, we don't even know if we are going to be alive tomorrow. So, make this 24 hours your best 24 hours ever.

Questions for Further Growth

Do you know for sure how long forever is to you?

_____

_____

_____

_____

Have you stayed sober for 24 hours in the past?

_____

_____

_____

What will you do for the next 24 hours to ensure you do not engage in your addiction? If you can do this for 24 hours, the opportunities are endless!

_____

_____

_____

_____

Today I will embrace the reality that NOW is all life truly is.

Tip #50: Exercise is Good for the Brain

"It is exercise alone that supports the spirits, and keeps the mind in vigor."

Marcus Tullius Cicero

Exercise is one of the most effective coping strategies and mood enhancers that we can possibly practice. Our "feel good" brain chemicals are activated and increase enormously during exercise. Our brains release dopamine, endorphins, and other chemicals that kill pain, produce pleasure, and give us energy when we exercise. It's a win-win; we get more energy, improve our moods, raise our self-esteem, and increase our physical health. People often overlook exercise because it is simple but it does much more than a lot of medications we take for physical and psychological purposes. Make sure you experiment with different exercises and make it fun. You will love it and be amazed at the effects it has on your life.

Questions for Further Growth

Are you taking care of your physical being in the recovery process?

_____

_____

_____

_____

Experiment with some form of exercise today and report back to document your experience.

_____

_____

_____

_____

What are some physical exercises or activities that you have always wanted to do? What's holding you back? Go get it!

_____

_____

_____

_____

Today I will make a commitment to add regular exercise to my recovery plan and make my life a healthy adventure.

Tip #51: Co-Occurring Disorders

"You are not your illness. You have an individual story to tell. You have a name, a history, a personality. Staying yourself is part of the battle."

Julian Seifter

Current research has demonstrated that a large percentage of people suffering from addiction also suffer from other disorders, including, but not limited to, major depressive disorder, anxiety disorders, bipolar disorder, post-traumatic stress disorder, and many others. We must seek treatment and manage these right along with our addiction to have the best chance at recovery. It's theorized that we often self-medicate these illnesses with our addiction. Relapse is much more common and consistent for those who do not seek treatment for their co-occurring disorders.

Questions for Further Growth

Do you have or do you think you may have another mental illness along with your addiction?

_____

_____

_____

_____

Is this illness being treated or have you sought appropriate help?

_____

_____

_____

_____

Do you define yourself by these labels?

_____

_____

_____

_____

Today I will be sure I am treating my entire being.

Tip #52: What's Your Purpose?

"The mystery of human existence lies not in just staying alive, but in finding something to live for."

Fyodor Dostoyevsky

What motivates you to get out of bed each day and do your absolute best in life? Can you honestly and thoroughly answer this question? If not, you must begin searching for your purpose once you have some stability in recovery. Doing something that gives you meaning and passion each day is one of the best defenses against relapse. What do you love, what do you want to accomplish? Start exploring these questions in your life and find the reason why you are on this earth. Rest assured there is an inner genius that is waiting to be fulfilled. Once you find this you will have guidance and direction to get through anything in your life. A psychiatrist named Victor Frankl who was a holocaust survivor and wrote many books said, "Those who have a 'why' to live can bear with almost any 'how'."

Questions for Further Growth

What did you dream of accomplishing as a child?

_____

_____

_____

_____

If you woke up tomorrow morning and your life was perfect what would that specifically look like?

_____

_____

_____

_____

If you knew you would not fail in your quest toward a major goal what would this be?

_____

_____

_____

_____

Today I will search for my deeper purpose in life.

Tip #53: Put One Foot Forward

"You simply have to put one foot in front of the other and keep going. Put blinders on and plow right ahead."

George Lucas

Many days in recovery come down to simply putting one foot in front of the other and focusing on moving forward, or at least not moving backward. No analyzing, no beating yourself up, no obsessing, just walking the straight path of recovery knowing that everything is going to be okay. We are in this thing for the long haul so not every day needs to be ground breaking with amazing feats being performed. Long journeys begin with a single step and continue one step at a time. So, if you're having one of those days, shut your mind down to the best of your ability, don't make any big decisions, and just walk.

Questions for Further Growth

What is stopping you from simply persisting along the path of recovery?

_____

_____

_____

_____

_____

Do you have the ability to put one foot in front of the other one day at a time?

_____

_____

_____

_____

Do you think this strategy is too simple for you?

_____

_____

_____

_____

*Today I will simply put one foot in front of the other
and know that I am growing.*

Tip #54: Acceptance is the Answer

"And acceptance is the answer to all my problems today. When I am disturbed, it is because I find some person, place, thing or situation — some fact of my life — unacceptable to me, and I can find no serenity until I accept that person, place, thing or situation as being exactly the way it is supposed to be at this moment."

Alcoholics Anonymous Big Book (pg. 449)

Acceptance is one of the greatest tools we can utilize in recovery and life. We must limit our habitual need to fight everyone and everything. I know we have been conditioned by society to do this, but we must start to change. We seem to love to bang our heads against the wall repeatedly for no apparent reason. Most of the things in our life beyond our own behavior cannot be changed. Acceptance is our answer to peace and serenity. This certainly doesn't mean we must like the things we accept.

Questions for Further Growth

What areas of your life are you currently resisting and banging your head against the wall repeatedly?

_____

_____

_____

_____

Have you done everything you can in your power to change this situation?

_____

_____

_____

_____

How can you use The Serenity Prayer to help situations that you are stuck in?

_____

_____

_____

_____

*Today I will assess my life and decide what requires
the practice of acceptance.*

Tip #55: Suffering-Use It!

"Out of suffering have emerged the strongest souls; the most massive characters are seared with scars."

Kahlil Gibran

Your agony and suffering caused by addiction is an indication that it is time to change and create a new life. We are not put on this earth to suffer and when suffering takes over our life, it is warning that change must come. Our suffering is a sign that it is time to give up what we are doing and seek a different path. You truly do not have to suffer anymore. Right now is the time to free yourself and begin to live a life of productivity and happiness. A new life is yours to create if you make the decision with your entire being. Choose it now and you will see the many resources available to help you. Once you begin to change, you will see how the whole universe will jump in and stand in your corner supporting you in everything you do. It's simply up to you to say, "I'm done with this shit. It's time to change."

Questions for Further Growth

What have you learned from your personal suffering?

_____

_____

_____

_____

Are you ready to surrender and live an amazing life filled with integrity?

_____

_____

_____

_____

What changes do you believe you need to make right now in your recovery?

_____

_____

_____

_____

Today I will use my suffering to achieve success.

Tip #56: HOW-Honesty, Open-mindedness, and Willingness!

"Are you willing to do absolutely anything to live an unimaginable existence?"

Richard Singer

There are three indispensable characteristics of recovery that we must always embrace. They are the "HOW" of recovery and you will get nowhere without them. In fact, life in general requires these as well. Honesty, open-mindedness, and willingness are our keys to the recovery process. All growth and progress in recovery is built on a strong foundation of these three principles. We must first be honest with ourselves, stop thinking we know everything, and be willing to consistently take positive action. People who don't achieve recovery are failing in at least one of these areas.

Questions for Further Growth

How are you practicing self-honesty in your life today?

_____

_____

_____

_____

How is the characteristic of willingness alive in your recovery right now?

_____

_____

_____

_____

Are you being truly openminded and not just open according to your beliefs?

_____

_____

_____

_____

Today I will assess myself based on the
principles of honesty, open-mindedness and willingness.

Tip #57: Daily Reflections

"Positive thinking is powerful thinking. If you want happiness, fulfillment, success and inner peace, start thinking you have the power to achieve those things. Focus on the bright side of life and expect positive results."

Germany Kent

I find it extremely helpful to utilize a meditation or reflection book in the morning to provide me with something to reflect on throughout the day. There are tons of great books out there you can buy or download. This is a very simple practice that provides guidance all day long.

Questions for Further Growth

Do you currently have a morning routine of reflection, prayer or meditation that helps you start your day with positive intentions?

_____

_____

_____

_____

What type of literature would you find helpful to start a morning ritual?

_____

_____

_____

_____

How do you think a morning reflection can benefit your recovery?

_____

_____

_____

_____

_____

Today I will start my day with a positive intention
and look back on it throughout my 24-hour journey.

Tip #58: Laugh at Yourself

"More important than talent, strength, or knowledge is the ability to laugh at yourself and enjoy the pursuit of your dreams."

Amy Grant

There's a saying that I love and it makes so much sense to me, "Don't take life too seriously, no one gets out alive." I know if I don't practice this in my life I can easily create drama and disasters daily. If I am not careful I make everything into a catastrophe. Remember this and practice laughing at yourself and life on a regular basis. We must find humor in life to survive and tap into the joy we deserve. Laugh regularly, nothing is as bad as you make it out to be.

Questions for Further Growth

What areas of your life do you take much too seriously?

_____

_____

_____

_____

What are some examples of humor in your life right now?

_____

_____

_____

_____

How can you add some laughter and joy to your recovery?

_____

_____

_____

_____

Today I will notice the humor in my life and the world around me.

Tip #59: Your Positive Attributes

"Self-love is not the process of ignoring your flaws.
Self-love is expanding your awareness to include your flaws and your strengths."
Vironika Tugaleva

Sometimes in recovery we get so caught up in a pattern of looking at all our negative qualities, yet we must look at the many positive qualities that we possess as well. I know the people with addictions I treated were some of the most creative, intelligent, caring, and overall incredible people I've ever met. You have a ton of positive attributes. Make a list of these positive qualities and embrace them daily.

Questions for Further Growth

What are some of your positive traits that you often overlook?

_____

_____

_____

_____

Ask 3 people in your life for at least three of your positive characteristics and write them down.

_____

_____

_____

_____

How do you plan on using these characteristics in a unique and helpful way in your new life?

_____

_____

_____

_____

Today I will focus on my strengths and make use of them in my recovery.

Tip #60: Personal Relapse Contract

"Sometimes relapse doesn't seem like that much of a threat,
but nobody is guaranteed to live through their next one."

Josie Tuttle

I suggest preparing a relapse contract and sharing it with the people in your life. List the consequences that will take place if you choose to relapse. Make sure you are detailed and honest about what you know will happen. Along with the consequences, list the actions your family should take and then sign the contract. Your signature states that you are consciously choosing these consequences and you accept what happens from there. This can be a powerful exercise for your recovery and may just allow you to stop and think before you choose to take a step back into hell. Relapse may not always seem like a choice; however, the fact is that we are the ones who decide to take that first addictive action.

Questions for Further Growth

What are some of the major consequences you will face if you choose to relapse?

_____

_____

_____

_____

_____

_____

What are you willing to do as far as treatment goes if you relapse?

_____

_____

_____

_____

_____

_____

_____

_____

*Today I will choose to keep what is good in my life
and not return to the destruction of addiction.*

The Essential Addiction Recovery Companion 63

Tip #61: New Day, New Life

"Each new day is a blank page in the diary of your life.
The secret of success is in turning that diary into the best story you possibly can."
Douglas Pagels

Each day we wake up we are given a whole new life to do what we want. One of my favorite sayings by Gandhi states, "Each night when I go to sleep I die and the next morning when I wake up, I am reborn." We are born each day to live spontaneously and be the person we desire to be. We don't have to allow the past or future to rule our lives. It's a conscious choice. We can live life as if it were a daily gift or live how we were conditioned to live and suffer. That's the bottom line!

Questions for Further Growth

Describe the person you yearn to be?

_____

_____

_____

_____

What is holding you back from making the most of the one precious life you were given?

_____

_____

_____

_____

How will you start your new life today? What is a good personal motto for your renewed life?

_____

_____

_____

_____

_____

*Today I will face life with passion and vigor and
be grateful for another chance to grow.*

Tip #62: Spontaneity

"You can devise all the plans in the world, but if you don't welcome spontaneity; you will just disappoint yourself."

Abigail Biddinger

I mentioned this in the tip above but I want to expand on it a bit further. We spend most of our lives living according to society, our past, and what we have been conditioned to believe we are supposed to do. This is not freedom and it's not genuinely living. Experiment with spontaneity and do your absolute best to refrain from what society desires. Escape your past identity and be who you are now. Allow your heart to guide you and be the person you always desired to be. I believe in you and know you are an incredibly special and unique human being.

Questions for Further Growth

What is stopping you from taking advantage of the freedom you have?

_____

_____

_____

_____

Look back on your plans in the past. Did they work out as you wanted at the time?

_____

_____

_____

_____

_____

What will you do today to celebrate your freedom and embrace spontaneity in your life?

_____

_____

_____

_____

_____

Today I will not follow the majority; I will follow my heart and soul.

Tip #63: Grieving

"No rule book. No time frame. No judgment. Grief is as individual as a fingerprint. Do what is right for your soul."

Anonymous

We deal with grief in our lives when losing anything or anyone. As part of recovery, we will certainly be grieving our addiction and we need to allow ourselves to proceed through the stages. The stages identified in the grieving process are: *denial, anger, bargaining, depression and acceptance*. It doesn't mean you are going to go through these in order but these are the stages you will experience and ultimately you will come to accept the loss in your life and return to a stable path. Give yourself time to grieve and remember these stages when you experience loss in your life. Anytime change occurs and something is missing from our lives, we tend to go through the grieving process. Be patient and kind to yourself as you grieve.

Questions for Further Growth

Are their people in your life that you have lost that you have not entirely grieved?

_____

_____

_____

_____

Are you grieving the loss of your addiction?

_____

_____

_____

_____

What stage of grief do you believe you are currently in concerning the losses mentioned above?

_____

_____

_____

_____

Today I will embrace where I am in the grieving process and know that I am doing the absolute best I can at this very moment.

Tip #64: Stop Believing the Lies

"Before you can break out of prison you must realize you are locked up."

Unknown

Addiction is the master of fabricating lies to keep you in its destructive cycle and ultimately take your life. You can sit back and observe these lies and choose to let them go without feeding into them. Addiction will remain a constant liar, but the lies tend to decrease and eventually go away if you allow them to. This is the only choice if you desire to have a new life and long-term recovery. Feeding into these lies and allowing them to take you over will always lead back to your addiction.

Make a comprehensive list of the lies that your addiction tells you and be prepared to challenge them and release them when they sneak up on you. Some of my addiction's lies include things such as, "You can just have a few drinks", "What about just smoking pot?" "Are you sure you're an addict?" "Most of these recovery things don't work, maybe I can just do it on my own," and they just continue on and on. Don't let your addiction fool you anymore.

Questions for Further Growth

What are some of the lies that addiction communicates to you?

_____

_____

_____

_____

_____

_____

What are some key "truths" that can challenge these lies when they reoccur?

_____

_____

_____

_____

_____

Today I will face the truth and stop believing
the lies created by addiction.

Tip #65: Humility is Vital

"It is unwise to be too sure of one's own wisdom.
It is healthy to be reminded that the strongest might weaken and the wisest might err."

Mahatma Gandhi

A simple definition of humility from Webster's dictionary is, "not thinking you are better than others." We must embrace humility and understand that we are all equal and we travel through this thing called life together. We are in the same boat! Believing the delusion that you are better than anyone or less than anyone will sabotage your recovery in a split second. When we begin to compare ourselves to anybody rather than relating as human beings, we enter an unhealthy state of mind. Ultimately, we were all created the same way and we all end the same way. If we live that truth and genuinely relate to other human beings as extensions of ourselves, we will have a healthy life.

Questions for Further Growth

Do you often compare yourself or your recovery to others?

_____

_____

_____

_____

Do you feel inferior to or superior to others on a regular basis?

_____

_____

_____

_____

How do you practice humility in your recovery?

_____

_____

_____

_____

Today I will think of myself less and act as an extension of humanity.

Tip #66: Obstacles as Opportunities

"It still holds true that man is most uniquely human when he turns obstacles into opportunities."
Eric Hoffer

There are always going to be obstacles in our path, but they only become problems when we perceive them that way. In every so-called obstacle, there is an opportunity for growth. There's an incredible book by Ryan Holiday called *Obstacle is the Way*. I suggest you read this carefully and turn your obstacles into great opportunities in your life. As I discussed before, it is all about our perception. If we change our perception, we change our life.

Questions for Further Growth

What obstacles are you currently facing in your life?

_____

_____

_____

_____

_____

_____

Take one of them now and reframe it into an opportunity for growth and further success.

_____

_____

_____

_____

_____

_____

_____

_____

Today I will reframe obstacles in my life as opportunities
for growth and transformation.

Tip #67: HALT-Are You Hungry, Angry, Lonely or Tired?

"Fortunately, hunger, anger, loneliness, and tiredness are easy to address and serve as a warning system before things reach a breaking point."

Unknown

In recovery, HALT is a wonderful acronym to always keep in mind. When we are not feeling right throughout the day, HALT can be used as a quick assessment to figure out what may be going on within us. HALT stands for HUNGRY, ANGRY, LONELY, TIRED. If you're struggling, you may be hungry, angry, lonely or tired. These are major areas that can mess with our moods, motivation, energy levels, and overall feelings of well-being. I know for me this almost always applies when I feel like shit. Fix the area that's faulty and you will feel much better. Seems quite simple but it works very well. I've come to realize that a lot of recovery is applying very simple techniques and keeping things as simple as possible.

Questions for Further Growth

Do you have a habit of making recovery overly complicated?

_____

_____

_____

_____

What are some other simple strategies that you can begin to practice daily to simplify your life?

_____

_____

_____

_____

HALT now and assess if you are Hungry, Angry, Lonely or Tired? Make this a habit!

_____

_____

_____

_____

Today and everyday forward I will remember to HALT in order to quickly resolve any challenging moments on my journey.

Tip #68: Living in Balance-The Middle Way

"The middle path is the way to wisdom."

Rumi

This is an enormous change for me. I consistently lived my life trapped in extremes. I spent much of my life with two feelings; loving life and feeling euphoric or hating life and wanting to fucking die. I either functioned amazingly well or couldn't function at all. A vital aspect of recovery is working to have balance in our lives. In Buddhism, this is referred to *The Middle Way*. It's the path between the two extremes. We need to work at being okay with simply being okay. Highs and lows always have their consequences. Balance and simplicity go a long way in recovery and creating our new lives.

Questions for Further Growth

Are you okay simply sitting by yourself for an hour doing absolutely nothing?

_____

_____

_____

_____

What extremes are a part of your life on a regular basis?

_____

_____

_____

_____

Sit alone with yourself for a half hour today and describe your experience. Just BE!

_____

_____

_____

_____

_____

Today I will find immense peace in being simply "okay". I can just BE!

Tip #69: Cognitive Strategies

"The world as we have created it is a process of our thinking.
It cannot be changed without changing our thinking."

Albert Einstein

Our thinking is a little flawed when we enter recovery, to say the least, and it remains that way for quite some time. There's a field of therapy called Cognitive Therapy that we can practice in our daily lives. It consists of challenging and changing our thoughts to change our feelings and behaviors. Our thoughts lead to feelings and then, obviously, our feelings lead to our behaviors so if we can intervene at the thought level we can alter our feelings and make smart decisions about our behavior. We have irrational and self-defeating thoughts that we need to be aware of so they can be challenged and changed. Pay attention to your thoughts and beliefs and work on changing the ones that are extremely irrational and self-defeating. It's helpful to write them down in a journal so you become familiar with them and can plan your attack before they come. I suggest that you research Cognitive Therapy and learn a little about it. It works!

Questions for Further Growth

What are some irrational thinking patterns that you recognize in your life?

_____

_____

_____

_____

_____

_____

_____

Write down a specific irrational thought or belief that you are aware of and then write down some ways you can challenge or reframe this thought or belief.

_____

_____

_____

_____

_____

Today I will work on challenging my negative thinking patterns.

Tip #70: There is No Comparison

"The best feeling in the world is watching things fall into place after watching them fall apart for so long."

Unknown

There's no chance that my addiction to drugs, alcohol and other behaviors could even compare to the life I live today. There's nothing addiction can offer me and I promise you if you are persistent and dedicated in your recovery efforts there will come a time when getting high will have nothing to offer you either. Any perceived benefit from your addiction will never compare to what you feel in recovery. Your life will consist of what you desire and so much more. You will feel more euphoric than you ever did from artificial chemicals or behaviors, you will have no fear, you will have meaning and purpose, and you will feel connected. You will go far beyond the feeling that your addiction ever provided you. You will get there eventually. I promise and it won't take that long.

Questions for Further Growth

What did your addiction give you that you were willing to lose your life over?

_____

_____

_____

_____

_____

_____

What specific feelings do you hope to have in recovery that you don't have right now?

_____

_____

_____

_____

_____

_____

Today I will believe in the ultimate power of recovery to completely renovate my life.

Tip #71: Act as If

"Act as if you are the person you want to be."

Bernie Siegel

"Act as If" is a remarkable strategy I discovered in my recovery. Some people may say it's faking; I see it as an innovative and creative strategy to act myself into a new life. It's my behavioral change strategy and I know it works. Act as if you are already that happy, successful person in recovery living all your dreams. It's effective in all areas of life. I used it successfully throughout my career acting my way into higher positions, acting as if I was an author, and so on. I get creative with it to the point of visualizing myself where I want to be, dressing the part and changing my behavior to the behavior of the specific role I wish to acquire. Give it a shot!

Questions for Further Growth

What specific characteristics do you hope to develop in your recovery?

_____

_____

_____

_____

What are some of your short-term goals?

_____

_____

_____

_____

_____

Where do you want to be in the future? Visualize it in detail and begin to act the part now?

_____

_____

_____

_____

_____

Today I will "act as if" I am the person I aspire to be.

Tip #72: Beginner's Mind

"A man ceases to be a beginner in any given science and becomes a master in that science when he has learned that he is going to be a beginner all his life."

Robin G. Collingwood

My relapse after being clean for 15 years taught me that I must always remain a beginner and completely open minded. Once you think you got this, that's when you are in serious shit. Being humble and realizing I don't know very much is where I will remain now after that torturous learning experience. If you think about it, no one knows too much compared to the amount of knowledge available in this world. In fact, I realize that as I get older I know much less than I once thought I did. Experience recovery as a beginner and you are well on your way. None of us have this licked and we never will. It's a daily process. Remember, pride comes before the fall.

Questions for Further Growth

Do you believe your immense knowledge of addiction and recovery is going to keep you sober forever?

_____

_____

_____

_____

_____

_____

How do you practice being a beginner in your recovery?

_____

_____

_____

_____

_____

_____

_____

_____

Today I will remain a student and be teachable
in all aspects of my life.

Tip #73: Cross-Addiction is Real

"I was not addicted to a specific substance.
I was addicted to more of whatever would take me out of myself."

Richard Singer

Take this one from me without having to do your own experimentation or "Field Work". I've done enough for everyone and taking it from me will save you a lot of pain and suffering. Due to our brain chemistry and biochemical makeup, we cannot safely use any mind altering chemical or engage in high risk behaviors. There are two things that will happen if you choose to go this route and not heed my warning. You will either become addicted to the alternative behaviors and chemicals or you will go back to your addiction of choice.

I realize your mind does not want to believe this and you may want to believe that having a few drinks will not do any harm, but I'm telling you ahead of time that it leads to disastrous consequences. I urge you to end this cycle now and accept that you will never successfully "get high" without falling into the trap of addiction. It's just not biologically possible. It has absolutely nothing to do with your will.

Questions for Further Growth

Have you experienced the powerful phenomenon of cross addiction? Explain.

_____

_____

_____

_____

_____

_____

Do you still feel like you are the "unique one" that is going to beat this without changing your life?

_____

_____

_____

_____

_____

_____

Today I will internalize the fact that I will become addicted
to anything that alters my mind and allows me to escape reality.

Tip #74: Disease or Not?

"Addiction is the only disease that tells you that you do not have a disease."

Jason Powers, MD

There's a long standing and emotion filled debate in the field of addiction about whether it is a disease or not. I don't want to get involved in that because it's not productive at all. However, it's good to know that the American Medical Association defined it a disease in the 1950's and recently updated its definition. Currently in the scientific community, addiction is categorized as a brain disorder. I would suggest doing your own research and learning a little about addiction science. Either way, it's obvious to me that addiction is certainly an illness and not a choice.

Absolutely no one wakes up and says I want to be an addict and ruin my entire life. That's ridiculous and pathetic to even theorize. Bottom line is we have an illness that requires targeted and individualized treatment to recover from. In the end, we need to do what we must do regardless of the definition of addiction. For you and me, it doesn't matter what the definition is. The what and why of addiction will never keep us in recovery, but some knowledge is helpful to us and our acceptance level.

Questions for Further Growth

Do you see addiction as disease or illness? Why or why not?

_____

_____

_____

_____

_____

_____

What is your addiction to you? Do you believe you need to treat it daily?

_____

_____

_____

_____

_____

_____

Today I will recognize that I have an illness that must be treated daily.

Tip #75: Integrate Altruism into Your Life

"Altruism is the best source of happiness. There is no doubt about that."

His Holiness, The Dalai Lama

Altruism is simply doing something without expecting anything in return. As Gandhi said, "Be the change you wish to see in the world." All change begins with us. Start by doing something nice for someone and don't tell anyone. It's an exhilarating feeling. This is the true art of giving. Just doing something simple like paying for someone's bill who's behind you in the drive thru can go a long way. Think of some acts of kindness you can participate in and you will be astounded at the effect it has on you and the people around you. Why live if we don't give?

Questions for Further Growth

Have you been helped by others kindness in the past? How?

_____

_____

_____

_____

_____

What feelings do you experience when you help others?

_____

_____

_____

_____

_____

What will you do today to help without telling anyone?

_____

_____

_____

_____

_____

Today I will add a random act of kindness into my daily plan.

Tip #76: Share Your Story

"Tears are words that need to be written."

Paulo Coelho

In our technology-filled world, there are so many ways we can share our stories to motivate someone else and pass on a little hope. You never know whose life you can save by giving a little of yourself and letting people know that there is hope in darkness. You can also simply write it down and share it with others in your life. The important thing is to share it. It will inspire others and it helps you to remember where you were and where you never want to return.

Questions for Further Growth

What about your story can change others' lives?

_____

_____

_____

_____

_____

_____

Where will you share your story to make the most impact?

_____

_____

_____

_____

_____

What is the unique title of your life story?

_____

_____

_____

_____

Today I will begin to write my story so I can change someone else's life by sharing my unique perspective.

Tip #77: Act Without Thinking

"The distance between your dreams and reality is called action."

Unknown

This strategy has helped me immensely in my recovery and all aspects of my life. It's simply acting without thinking about it for very long. I'm certainly not talking about acting impulsively but acting in healthy ways, such as going to therapy, or a support group, or even going to the gym. It helps me with simply getting out of bed some days. Often when we think about things too much we think ourselves out of doing them. I jump out of bed without thinking about hitting snooze or just go to the gym without pondering the benefits and the energy it's going to take. Get up and act! It's often said we must act ourselves into a new way of living. Actions will change your life. Our mind often enjoys thinking ourselves out of productive activities; don't let your mind win!

Questions for Further Growth

What things in your recovery could be done without thinking?

_____

_____

_____

_____

_____

_____

Has overthinking really helped you to get anywhere? Explain.

_____

_____

_____

_____

_____

Today I will take action rather than be possessed by my mind.

Tip #78: Just Don't Pick Up

"Don't pick up the first drink and you won't get drunk."

Unknown

A very simple yet effective concept in recovery is that if you don't pick up the first drink, drug, or engage in the behavior, you have nothing to worry about. Some days, that's all you need to concentrate on: not picking up the first one. Keep it that simple for the day. Tell yourself, I'm not going to use or engage in an addictive behavior today and that's enough. Some days, that's all you are going to accomplish and that's success. You win today and you can work on other things tomorrow. There's plenty of hope for the future if you don't fall back into your addiction today. It's a miracle for us addicts to be in recovery 24 hours and that's all that is ever asked of us.

Questions for Further Growth

What would a drink, drug or other addictive behavior provide you right now that you don't already possess?

_____

_____

_____

_____

Do simple strategies in recovery bother you or make you doubtful?

_____

_____

_____

_____

Do you believe you are a complete success if your addiction free today? Why or why not?

_____

_____

_____

_____

*Today I will not pick up or engage in addictive behavior
no matter what!*

Tip #79: Become a Student

"Seeking knowledge is like opening doors. And I know the doors are everywhere."
Georges St-Pierre

In my personal life, I have found it exceptionally helpful to become a student of recovery and addiction. Try doing some research on addiction, recovery, and relapse prevention. You certainly don't have to go as far as I did. I kind of made a life out of it but I guess that's what I needed. Just by being a student, I've been able to use my knowledge and experience to help people in ways I never thought possible. I think just doing a little bit of it can help you immensely in your life. Becoming a student of our passions can be an awesome experience, so do it with recovery related information as well as other things you are curious about. Being a student has enlightening benefits and you will always remain open to the knowledge of life.

Questions for Further Growth

What curiosities do you have about addiction?

_____

_____

_____

_____

What knowledge about recovery would be most helpful to you?

_____

_____

_____

_____

_____

What are you passionate about that you would love to know more about?

_____

_____

_____

_____

*Today I will seek knowledge about recovery
and take action toward a better life.*

Tip #80: Investigate Spirituality

"The door is wide and open, don't go back to sleep."

Rumi

Remember, religion and spirituality are two different things. Religion is manmade and spirituality is an innate part of our beings. Investigate your own spirituality or spiritual feelings and write down what you discover. Answer these questions: *Is there something more or bigger than you? How was the universe created? What are some qualities of your higher power if you currently have one?* Also, research different religions and forms of spirituality and see what you find within them. Try to build your own unique spirituality. Personally, I read whatever I could get my hands on and continue to create my personal spiritual philosophy. My spirituality is constantly evolving. Spirituality is very personal and unique to each of us. Discover yours!

Questions for Further Growth

Is there something more or higher than you?

_____

_____

_____

_____

How do you believe the Universe was created?

_____

_____

_____

_____

What are some qualities of your higher power?

_____

_____

_____

_____

Today I will awaken the spirit within me.

Tip #81: Be Grateful

"Cultivate the habit of being grateful for every good thing that comes to you, and to give thanks continuously. And because all things have contributed to your advancement, you should include all things in your gratitude."

Ralph Waldo Emerson

We need to remain grateful for what we have and appreciate being alive. Gratitude is the most powerful attitude we can possess in recovery. A grateful addict has no need to go back to their addiction. If you think about it, you have an infinite number of things to be grateful for. Just think of those who have much less than you. Keep in mind there are people who don't know where their next meal will come from, can't locate clean drinking water, have no home, have no legs, and that's just a few examples. There is always someone much worse off than you.

Make it a habit to write down what you are grateful for and take it a step further and express your gratitude to those you love. We get caught up in life and forget how good we have it. We start whining about luxury issues while people are being killed and tortured in other areas of the world. Always remember there are real problems and luxury problems. Please don't moan about luxury issues.

Questions for Further Growth

Make a gratitude list! What are you grateful for today?

_____

_____

_____

_____

_____

_____

_____

_____

_____

_____

_____

_____

_____

_____

Today I will simply be grateful for where I am and what I have.

Tip #82: Mindfulness Matters

"With mindfulness, you can establish yourself in the present in order to touch the wonders of life that are available in that moment."

Thich Nhat Hahn

Practicing mindfulness has become extremely popular due to the benefits it has on all aspects of our health. It has been around for thousands of years and we are just now catching up with it. In the west, we have the bad habit of being very closed minded which blocks us from a lot of amazing alternative strategies. Mindfulness is very simple and fits perfect with recovery. It simply asks us to stay completely in the moment without judging our thoughts and feelings. Just noticing what is going on inside and outside of us and being there. Just be and experience the only moment that is available to us, the *Now*. This can be done in every waking moment of our lives. No need to stop and sit down or find a cave in the mountains. It's just simply being intimate with life. I suggest researching mindfulness a little and becoming friends with this effective way of living. Keep in mind it takes practice and your mind will resist it but it does get easier as you continuously and persistently bring your being back to the moment.

Questions for Further Growth

Practice mindful journaling. Get in the Now and write down what you see around you, what you are currently feeling and what thoughts are going through your head. Do this all while simply observing the moment and not attaching or judging anything in your experience. Where do you live most of your life: Past, Present or Future?

_____

_____

_____

_____

_____

_____

_____

_____

_____

_____

_____

Today I will embrace the NOW of life and know that
life only consists of this unique and precious moment.

Tip #83: FEAR! What Will You Choose?

"Ultimately we know deeply that the other side of every fear is freedom."

Mary Ferguson

Fear is said to represent two opposing options concerning our recovery and our new life: Face Everything And Recover or Fuck Everything And Run. Fear often runs every aspect of our lives without us even realizing it. We must face the fear inside us and become aware of how it is affecting our lives. It is impossible to live a genuine life if we are constantly living in fear. It is said that all fear comes from our ultimate fear of death. Thus, fear becomes involved in everything we do. We fear success and fear failure, we fear people and fear being lonely, we fear our addiction and fear recovery, and so on. It is imperative that we become aware of our fears and power through them to experience freedom and joy in recovery. There is no secret or complex psychological technique to work through fear. We simply must face the fear and do what we fear regularly and then it will subside.

Questions for Further Growth

What are some of your main fears?

_____

_____

_____

_____

_____

_____

Choose one of your fears today and make a commitment to begin facing it. Write about it in detail here.

_____

_____

_____

_____

_____

_____

_____

Today I will face everything and recover.

Tip #84: Willpower? No!

"If we could will ourselves out of addiction we would have done it a long time ago."

Unknown

People who are addicted have a tremendously powerful will, are extremely intelligent, creative, and true survivors. Just research a little and you will see the incredible human beings who are addicts in recovery or who have suffered at the hands of addiction. Our willpower is amazing in all aspects of our lives; however, it becomes useless when it comes to not engaging in our addiction. Of course, it comes in handy when participating in healthy recovery efforts, but in the direct act of stopping our use and behavior, it's as useless as trying to stop yourself from shitting yourself when you have diarrhea. Sorry about the grotesque and vivid example but I want to make my point clear. Believe me, if we could have *willed* or thought ourselves out of addiction, we would not need this book or any treatment for recovery. Please understand that you are not going to *will* yourself out of your addiction.

Questions for Further Growth

Have you tried to use will power in the past to not engage in your addiction? What were the results?

_____

_____

_____

_____

What are some things in your recovery that you can use your powerful will to do?

_____

_____

_____

_____

_____

_____

_____

_____

Today I will understand that I use my will to take action but it will never be enough on its own to remain in recovery.

Tip #85: Remember the Consequences in Detail

"Without reflection, we go blindly on our way, creating more unintended consequences, and failing to achieve anything useful."

Margaret J. Wheatley

I suggest that you recall in detail your last episode of addictive behavior so you don't return to that lifestyle. I would take it a step further and write down your five or more most destructive and painful moments that were a direct consequence of your addiction. Visualize this, including your feelings, your experiences, the people whose hearts were broken, and what you lost. Focus more on feelings and the internal and relational aspects that were lost, rather than material things. The material doesn't matter for the most part. It's the humanity we lose that devastates us. These consequences are waiting for you if you choose to release the beast of addiction back in your life. This monster runs through your life and the life of the ones you love creating disaster after disaster.

Questions for Further Growth

What do you recall about your last run with your addictive behavior or substance? What were the consequences, feelings and who did you harm? *Be specific and detailed so you can remember this and not return to it when your addiction attacks you next and tries to manipulate you into do it all over again!*

_____

_____

_____

_____

_____

_____

_____

_____

_____

_____

_____

_____

_____

Today I will choose not to repeat my past addictive behaviors.

Tip #86: Pride Comes Before the Fall

"Proud people breed sad sorrows for themselves."

Emily Brontë

I've experienced this personally and have observed many individuals brought to their knees due to their stubborn and unhealthy pride. Pride keeps us from reaching out for support and smugly declares, "I got this thing myself. What? So, you think I'm helpless? Leave me alone." This is never the case. We are social beings and need others' help on this journey. We all have our difficulties; no one is immune to the struggles of life. Keep in mind these three vital facts: *You will always need help, you don't know everything, and you will never have this illness licked.* The words "I got this" always comes before a relapse. Like I previously discussed, if your addiction is whispering you the *'I got this'* lie, please challenge this manipulation and reach out for help. Shine a light on the devious beast in your mind. Be humble, ask for help, and realize that the strong and courageous act is saying. "I need help." Those three simple words will save you from a repulsive and desperate existence and from a premature death at the hands of addiction.

Questions for Further Growth

Based on your experience and the fact that so many addicts are dying, do you ever think "I got this"?

_____

_____

_____

_____

_____

_____

What do you fear about becoming vulnerable and saying, "I need help"? There truly is no shame. The fight is over!

_____

_____

_____

_____

_____

_____

Today I will practice humility and allow myself to be vulnerable.

Tip #87: Stigma is Ignorant Bullshit

"In all my years as a physician, I have never, ever met an addicted person that wanted to be an addict."

Dr. Nora Volkow

Stigma surrounding addiction and recovery exists in this world whether we like it or not. It does not define who we are and we must not internalize it. It is a product of ignorance and delusion. It is our personal challenge and responsibility as human beings with addictions to disprove the beliefs that ignorant people continue to maintain about us. Personally, I've made it part of my purpose in life. To drop down to their level and argue with these ill-informed individuals is useless and a waste of our time and energy. If we live healthy lives and demonstrate the truth of addiction and recovery, the stigma will lose its power and eventually fade away. However, we must unite as a community and consistently speak out. My personal strategy is to get involved, educate, and work on developing community initiatives to view and talk about addiction and recovery in a different way.

Questions for Further Growth

What values has your addiction caused you to violate and compromise?

_____

_____

_____

_____

Write a description of who you truly are as a human being?

_____

_____

_____

_____

What will you do in your recovery to help fight the stigma created and maintained by society?

_____

_____

_____

_____

Today I will show society that I am not what the stigma defines me as.

Tip #88: Your Personal Vision Statement

"Personal leadership is the process of keeping your vision and values before you and aligning your life to be congruent with them."

Dr. Stephen Covey

Write a personal vision statement describing your mission for your new life. A detailed mission statement helps me to guide my behavior and prevents me from wandering away from the path I belong on. It is very simple and may change as you progress in your recovery. Right now, your only goal may be the all-important priority in your life, which is to stay clean and addiction free. This must be our number one priority or nothing else in life is possible. Once you have a strong foundation and stable recovery, you can then move on to your other aspirations. Be patient, the time will come and you are going to rock. My current personal vision is to inspire other human beings to change their lives and the world around them through my writing and actions in my life. What is yours?

Questions for Further Growth

Write your unique personal vision statement based on your passions and goals?

_____

_____

_____

_____

_____

_____

_____

_____

_____

_____

_____

_____

_____

Today I will begin writing the personal vision statement
that will guide my life and recovery.

Tip #89: Nutrition is Important

"The food you eat can be either the safest and most
powerful form of medicine or the slowest form of poison."

Ann Wigmore

You may not realize it, but what we ingest has an extensive impact on our recovery. I began to look further into this after reading an awesome book titled, *Recovery 2.0* by Tommy Rosen. He outlines a new paradigm for recovery from addictions. I suggest you take a look at it. Nutrition is often something we do on auto-pilot in our lives. Current research in the scientific community demonstrates that our habits of drinking and eating profoundly affect how our body responds to the environment and is immensely important to our energy levels, moods, cravings, and obviously, all aspects of our physical functioning. Start to focus some awareness on your eating and drinking habits. There's loads of resources out there to utilize but for now just drink a little more water and choose healthier foods without so much sugar. Keep it simple and just focus on little changes. You will feel the difference.

Questions for Further Growth

For one day make a list of your nutritional intake?

_____

_____

_____

_____

_____

_____

_____

_____

What changes would you like to make based on this initial assessment of your nutritional habits?

_____

_____

_____

_____

_____

*Today I will become aware of what I am putting in my body and
realize that part of my recovery is taking care of my body.*

Tip #90: We are as Sick as our Secrets!

"Nothing makes us so lonely as our secrets."

Paul Tournier

Secrets that are hidden in the darkness deep within us feed our addictions. We promised ourselves that they would never see the light of day, but the time has come to escape their bondage. I held on to a secret about a sexual assault that happened to me in the military and I vowed never to share it or reveal it in my life for as long as I live. This secret devoured my being for a very long time and nourished my addiction to the edge of death. I finally met a caring and compassionate therapist who gently pulled it out of me. Only then was I able to enjoy anything close to living as well as long-term recovery. Once I let go of this secret I was free. Since that time, I dedicated a great deal of time and energy on working with secrets that were holding people back from recovery. I had them write their secrets down and gently process them with me and then subsequently burned the motherfuckers. We must be willing to let our secrets go and no longer give them the power to plague our soul.

Questions for Further Growth

Do you have any deep dark secrets that you are holding inside?

_____

_____

_____

_____

Who do you trust enough to process these secrets with?

_____

_____

_____

_____

What are your fears about sharing these secrets?

_____

_____

_____

_____

Today I will take action to finally free myself of all my destructive secrets.

Tip #91: Slow the Hell Down!

"He that can have patience can have what he will."

Benjamin Franklin

We can learn from what Lao Tzu so eloquently expressed many years ago, *"Nature does not hurry, yet everything is accomplished."* If we can genuinely take this to heart in our recovery, we will discover that frantically running around trying to get everything done is useless and simply causes unnecessary anxiety. I know personally when my mind clears and I begin enjoying the gift of recovery I want to do everything at once and strive to accomplish all my dreams. I enter recovery and suddenly I want to be the president in a week. We are in this for the long haul. Recovery is a marathon not a sprint. Relax and take small steps daily and you will get big results. I promise.

Questions for Further Growth

What are you in a rush to do or achieve?

_____

_____

_____

_____

Has this frantic rushing behavior ever helped you in the past?

_____

_____

_____

_____

What are some strategies you can use to be patient and relax?

_____

_____

_____

_____

Today I will remember that rushing to somewhere in the future does not make time go faster; it simply causes unnecessary anxiety.

Tip #92: Guilt is a Healthy Feeling, but....

"I forgive myself and then I move on. You can sit there forever lamenting about how bad you have been, feeling guilty until you die, and not one tiny slice of that guilt will do anything to change a single thing in the past."

Dr. Wayne Dyer

Guilt is a normal, healthy feeling associated with things we've done in our addiction that we find unacceptable when we are clean. If you don't feel some guilt when entering recovery, it certainly is not a good sign. Sociopaths don't feel guilt, but I don't think you're a sociopath if you're reading this book focused on creating a life free from addiction. What is not healthy is feeling guilt over and over, 479,000 times. This is not necessary and not productive in your new life. Feeling this guilt and working on its resolution is a critical aspect of recovery. The goal is to change our behavior so we never have to feel this level of guilt again. Now that's freedom. Previously I discussed making amends for what we've done and making it up to those we hurt. This will help with your negative feelings and will create the freedom you desire. Guilt is like carrying around cement blocks everywhere we go. It's very enjoyable to release these and float along each day without this baggage holding us down.

Questions for Further Growth

What guilty feelings are you holding onto?

_____

_____

_____

_____

_____

Is this guilt helping you in your life or making you feel like you deserve to use? Guilt is a very deceptive feeling that feeds our illness.

_____

_____

_____

_____

_____

_____

Today I will not allow guilt to fuel my addiction
and create even more guilt in my life.

Tip #93: Watch for High Risk Behavior

"A High-Risk Situation is the last step in an ongoing relapse process."

Terrence Gorski

We absolutely must complete a risk assessment in our personal life concerning the high-risk factors that will lead us back to our old sinister existence. These high-risk factors are very personal and unique to you. When assessing these risks, keep in mind high-risk people, situations, places, music, and anything that may trigger your addictive behavior. These things can unconsciously lead to a relapse very quickly. They usually revolve around our five senses. Things we see, smell, taste, feel, and hear can trigger our desire to use. Our senses are powerful and when we associate things with the past, our brain yells, "I want to go back. I need to get high!" Our brains are programmed to form associations. We have deeply embedded triggers from many years of addiction. Take this step very seriously. You have many unique triggers in your life which you must meticulously assess to develop a plan for success. There are some helpful relapse prevention resources out there if you research them. Remember, become a student of recovery.

Questions for Further Growth

Are you on a path to a relapse according to your behavior or are you paving a solid road for recovery? *Focus on your behavior; your thoughts are always deceptive.*

_____

_____

_____

_____

_____

What behaviors have led you to relapse in the past?

_____

_____

_____

_____

_____

_____

_____

Today I will complete a thorough assessment of any possible high-risk situations and develop a plan to prevent these from interfering with my recovery.

Tip #94: Freedom of Choice

"Whether you think you can, or you think you can't—you're right."

Henry Ford

I often hear many people declare, "I can't get high. I can't get drunk. I can't do this. I can't do that!" You can do absolutely anything you desire. Personally, when someone tells me I can't do something, I like to show them that I can do what I please. We always have the choice to exist in our addiction or genuinely live in recovery. If your choice is to get drunk, high, or engage in some addictive behavior that's your choice. Just keep in mind that consequences come with each choice we make. I know very well that I can choose to get drunk or high. I have done it many times. What recovery has given me is the genuine desire to live a better life. That's a miracle for an addict like me.

Questions for Further Growth

What will you choose today: Life or death? Destruction or recovery?

_____

_____

_____

_____

How does it feel to have the freedom to choose whatever you truly desire today? Do you sincerely realize you can choose recovery and a transformed life? *Be brutally honest!*

_____

_____

_____

_____

_____

_____

_____

_____

_____

Today I will assert my freedom of choice and
choose what my heart truly desires.

Tip #95: Your Personal Bottom

"The view from rock bottom is often the reason, the inspiration, for getting back up."

Unknown

Hitting a bottom is a popular topic in treatment and recovery. Realistically, no set bottom exists. There's no such thing as a bottom in addiction unless we want to classify death as the definitive bottom because that's the lowest we can go. We personally decide the depth we wish to descend to. All so-called bottoms have a "trap door" and will always sink lower until death emerges. Right this moment, you have the choice to decide that your "bottom" will never go any lower. I quickly realized that I pulled out a shovel every relapse and dug deeper and deeper until I was as close to death as possible.

Questions for Further Growth

Have you hit a low enough bottom to put an end to the pain? Or do you feel like you need more pain until you're ready to get serious about this life or death business of recovery?

_____

_____

_____

_____

What does the scheming voice of addiction tell you about your bottom?

_____

_____

_____

_____

In your heart, do you really want to risk death or a deeper more painful bottom? *You must question your heart because your mind will always convince you to play the odds.*

_____

_____

_____

_____

Today I am grateful that I didn't hit the ultimate "Rock Bottom".

Tip #96: Music is Powerful

"Music produces a kind of pleasure which human nature cannot do without."

Confucius

Music can be an awfully powerful motivator in our lives, both in a negative and positive sense. In a positive sense, I choose songs that represent my recovery as well as motivate me in my journey of creating a new life. In a negative sense, music can trigger certain mindsets as well as a relapse. I choose what I listen to wisely. My theme song for recovery is *I'm not Afraid* by Eminem. This motivates and inspires me when I need it. Be careful with your music choice because it can creep up on you and trigger your brain to remember a time in the past associated with addiction. This is called state-dependent memory and it can be very devious. Most of the time, as addicts, we recall the pleasurable moments in our addiction and omit all the disastrous consequences. Be mindful of the small details in your recovery.

Questions for Further Growth

What are some songs that you need to recognize as possible triggers to addictive cravings?

_____

_____

_____

_____

_____

_____

What are some songs that may be possible anthems for your new life?

_____

_____

_____

_____

_____

_____

_____

_____

Today I will choose a musical anthem that motivates my recovery.

Tip #97: Eat Lots of Chocolate

"My therapist told me the way to achieve true inner peace is to finish what I start.
So far today, I have finished 2 bags of M&M's and a chocolate cake. I feel better already."

Dave Barry

Hopefully this isn't the only tip you will utilize, but I'm sure most of you readers will enjoy this one. Chocolate affects the same areas of the reward system in our brains that most addictions do. Eating chocolate helped me immensely with cravings in early recovery and the consequences aren't close to that of addiction. A little weight gain isn't a big deal; we can always exercise and eat healthily to curb this effect. Don't go way overboard but use this tip to appease your brain and body when it craves your addiction of choice. Enjoy!

Questions for Further Growth

What are some comfort foods or pleasurable activities you can utilize as a part of your recovery?

_____

_____

_____

_____

_____

_____

When you experiment with these foods monitor your thoughts and feelings and journal about the experience. Try it now with your favorite food and concentrate only on the moment. It is called *mindful eating*. Check it out online and use this strategy regularly.

_____

_____

_____

_____

_____

_____

_____

Today I will seek alternatives that satisfy cravings when they come.

Tip #98: Change Your Story

*"Every single step you take can, and will change your future. Your whole life is unwritten.
You're the author, make your story count."*

Nishan Panwar

Our lives consist of the detailed story we tell ourselves and others. We have the power to create a whole new story and terminate the manuscript of the past. *THE END*. That's all it takes and then we can begin writing our new story. We can also reframe our past story in a different way. For example, I reframe my past as a learning process that I had to endure to help others to change their lives for the better. We are truly free to write the story we desire and create whatever details and events we want in the new novel of our life.

Questions for Further Growth

How can you reframe your past to use it for good in the future?

_____

_____

_____

_____

What is the new title of your future story?

_____

_____

_____

_____

Right now, create the title of five new chapters in your future recovery story.

_____

_____

_____

_____

_____

_____

*Today I will reframe my past in a positive way
by finding a purpose within the negative.*

Tip #99: Let Go of the Little Dramas

"Don't let the silly little dramas of each day get you down.
For you are here to do great things."

Malika Nura

A large part of our lives consists of the fabricated little dramas we get drawn into. We get dragged along in this drama filled with delusions, lies, manipulations and nonsense that doesn't matter in the long run. You can escape this drama and abide in the truth, if you desire. Once we slow down and become aware of the unique moment in front of us, we begin to realize the truth and what genuinely matters. Excuse yourself from the drama in a friendly manner and begin focusing on what is important in your life, which begins with living a life free from addiction. Since I excused myself from the little dramas, my life has become much more joyous and free.

Questions for Further Growth

What type of drama do you often get dragged into and taken for the ride?

_____

_____

_____

_____

Look at these drama-filled situations clearly and ask yourself if they truly matter or will actually have any important effect on your life.

_____

_____

_____

_____

How can you prevent yourself from getting all worked up about senseless drama in the future?

_____

_____

_____

_____

Today I will detach from the drama around me and
immerse myself in the power of the present moment.

Tip #100: Never, Never, Never Give Up!

"Character consists of what you do on the third and fourth tries."

James A. Eichener

No matter what goes on in your recovery, do whatever it takes to continue moving forward. There will be obstacles, discomfort, and heartache. Of course, life won't always be fair, however I promise that being in recovery will never be as bad as being imprisoned in your addiction. You never have to rip the hearts out of those you love anymore. You will grow to love the gift of recovery. No temporary moment of pain, stress, or craving will be worth losing your new-found freedom. Never, never, never give up on recovery!

Questions for Further Growth

What in your life is currently being made a priority over your recovery?

_____

_____

_____

_____

What can you do when you get to the point of saying "Fuck it"?

_____

_____

_____

_____

Make a list of consequences you will face if you give up on your recovery?

_____

_____

_____

_____

_____

_____

Today I will promise myself to never give up on my #1 priority which is my recovery from addiction.

Tip #101: Feed Your Recovering Self

"No one can tell you how to feed your soul like your soul. Listen to it!"

Curtis Tyrone Jones

There's an awesome little story that I would like to share with you: One evening, an old Cherokee told his grandson about a battle that goes on inside people. He said, "My son, the battle is between two wolves inside us all." One is evil - he is anger, envy, sorrow, regret, greed, arrogance, self-pity, guilt, resentment, inferiority, lies, false pride, superiority, and ego." He continued, "The other is good—he is joy, peace, love, hope, serenity, humility, kindness, benevolence, empathy, generosity, truth, compassion, and faith. The same fight is going on inside you —and inside every other person, too." The grandson thought about it for a minute and then asked his grandfather, "Which wolf will win?" The old Cherokee simply replied, "The one you feed."

Questions for Further Growth

What are some things you need to do to stop feeding your addictive self?

_____

_____

_____

_____

_____

_____

What are some strategies you can use to be sure you feed your recovering self on a daily basis?

_____

_____

_____

_____

_____

_____

_____

Today, I will feed my recovery the proper nutrition to ensure that I never have to return to the torment of addiction.

Free Writing

Author's Final Note

Thank you for allowing me to enter your life in this small way. I hope you have enjoyed and discovered some benefit in this labor of love that helped me more than you can ever imagine. Please contact me at RSinger9999@gmail.com if you have any comments, questions or suggestions or if you just want to chat. In addition, I will always make myself available if you reach out of help with anything you are struggling with.

Remember, you can live a life beyond your wildest dreams one day at a time and with that you will touch the lives of human beings throughout this Universe in ways you could never imagine. Right now, you have the ability to leave your unique DENT on this miraculous and mysterious planet. That is a gift. Please accept it and use it wisely.

Namaste,

Rick

Index

101 Tips for Recovering from Addictions can help transform the life of any recovering addict from bleak to bright. These practical suggestions give hope, from seeing the light at the end of the tunnel, to realizing this light holds a promising future to reclaim. Readers will learn:

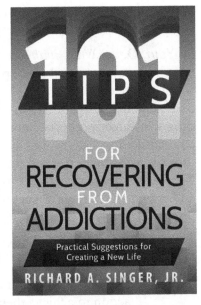

- How to keep hope and seek help, even in the darkest of days
- How to deal with the major monster of denial
- How to plan to become consistently productive
- How to take care of your brain and body so that you're happier and healthier
- How to routinely remember to never give up
- How to push through and know that recovery can be realized
- And much, much more

"*101 Tips for Recovering from Addictions* is a great resource, giving a simple, fun and easily digestible format to a treasure trove of accumulated wisdom from the Winners who have overcome addictions to have a happy and healthy life."

—Sarah Graham, addiction expert and
member of UK Advisory Council on the Misuse of Drugs (ACMD)

"*101 Tips For Recovering from Addiction* is a must read and a wonderful tool for anyone dealing with addictive behaviors and life's many waves. Rick Singer is writing from the heart and provides us with so many helpful strategies and coping skills! This book is a fantastic one to have in your hands!"

—Erica Spiegelman, Addiction Specialist, speaker and
author of *Rewired: A Bold New Approach to Addiction and Recovery*

"Having worked with people struggling with addictions for many years, I recognized many of the tools I regularly use among Rick Singer's *101 Tips for Recovering from Addictions* — I know they work. Therefore, I can confidently recommend this little book as inspiration, and as a guide."

—Bob Rich, Ph.D. author of several self-help and inspirational books

"*101 Tips for Recovering from Addictions* is a thoughtful, inspirational, must have for anyone in the addiction field or going through addiction themselves. Singer's own story is passionate, loving and realistic."

—Mari Sweeting, Recovery Coach, Substance Abuse Counselor and
DUI Instructor, Sonoma County, California

"*101 Tips for Recovering from Addictions* provides a safe space, a space to learn tools that will encourage personal strength as you explore within and work to overcome your addiction. With this book and personal dedication you can move towards freedom."

—Robin Marvel, author of
Framing a Family: Building a Foundation to Raise Confident Children

ISBN 978-1-61599-328-4

Loving Healing Press

Do you desire to change the world? It all starts with you so let's begin your transformation today!

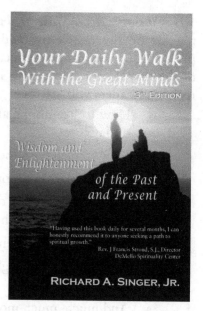

Your Daily Walk with the Great Minds is a daily journey based on psychological and spiritual principles that have been scientifically confirmed and shown to help create lasting change and personal growth. When each human being changes and grows it directly affects humanity. If each individual being is committed to change and self actualization the Universe will directly feel this peace and universal transformation will occur. There is no better time than Now to take part in Universal peace and enlightenment. Have you ever wondered?

- What your purpose and meaning in life is?
- How to combat anxiety and depression in your daily life?
- How to begin pursuing your dreams and taking action to achieve them?
- How to maintain peace of mind in a world of conflict and strife?
- How to transcend the monotony of daily life and truly embrace what life has to offer you?

I invite you to find the answers to these and other questions through meditations and journaling exercises on *Your Daily Walk with the Great Minds: Wisdom and Enlightenment of the Past and Present, 3rd Edition*

"Having used this book daily for several months, I can honestly recommend it to anyone seeking a path to spiritual growth."

--Rev. J Francis Stroud,
S.J., Director DeMello Spirituality Center

"I have spent my life studying lots and lots of self-development books and I can say emphatically that *Your Daily Walk with the Great Minds* ranks in the top ten. I whole heartedly recommend this book to any seeker of self-development."

--C. Kumarbabu, MD,
former chair of Psychiatry, Govt. Stanley Hospital, India

About the Author

Richard Singer is first of all a real human being who is quite faulty and still struggles with life on a daily basis, however on a worldly basis he is an award winning author, trained psychotherapist, Asst. Professor of Human and Social Science, and most importantly a seeker of truth. He continuously searches for wisdom to use in his life, as well as helping other human beings in their precious journey. He has studied Eastern Psychology, Buddhist Healing, and Non-Violence at the Doctoral Level; in addition, he has spent years devoted to the study of wisdom recorded throughout history. He seeks to impart this knowledge to the world through his writing.

ISBN 978-1-61599-114-3
Loving Healing Press